The A-Z of Curious

SUFFOLK

THE A-Z OF CURIOUS

SUFFOLK

SARAH E. DOIG

The
History
Press

*To my parents, who instilled in me a
curiosity in the people, places and events
around me, and who have encouraged and
supported all my endeavours.*

First published 2016

The History Press
The Mill, Brimscombe Port
Stroud, Gloucestershire, GL5 2QG
www.thehistorypress.co.uk

© Sarah E. Doig, 2016

The right of Sarah E. Doig to be identified as the Author
of this work has been asserted in accordance with the
Copyright, Designs and Patents Act 1988.

British Library Cataloguing in Publication Data.
A catalogue record for this book is available from the British Library.

ISBN 978 0 7509 6596 5

Typesetting and origination by The History Press
Printed and bound by CPI Group (UK) Ltd

Acknowledgements

Thank you to the people of Suffolk, present and past, for providing such a rich heritage. This book simply could not have been written without you.

There are a number of individuals who have provided information, offered suggestions on content, lent me books and magazines, and checked details of individual stories. Thank you, therefore, to Carolyn Boon, Stephen Dart, Chris Dunbavin, Caroline Hearn, Rosemary Knox, Neil Langridge, Diana Maywhort, Geoffrey Robinson, Jean Sheehan and 'The Eighth in the East'.

Thank you to staff at the Suffolk Record Office, in particular the Bury St Edmunds branch, for their enthusiastic help and support during my research. I would also like to pay tribute to Suffolk Libraries; an excellent service, without which I could simply not have accessed all the books I wanted to consult.

All the new, stunning location photographs in this book were taken by Tony Scheuregger. I am sure you will agree that they enhance the text tremendously. Thank you, Tony, for your skill and for your forbearance during our various trips racing around the Suffolk countryside.

There are also a number of people and organisations to whom I am extremely grateful for giving permission for me to reproduce prints and photographs. I have duly credited them by the relevant illustration. All other illustrations are, to the best of my knowledge, out of copyright.

Thank you to the staff at The History Press for turning my raw text and images into this finished product.

And last but definitely not least, I would like to thank my husband, Mike, who has provided support, offered advice, been a sounding board for my ideas, read through and commented on my initial drafts and generally kept the household running while I have been immersed in my writing.

Introduction

'Curiosity is, in great and generous minds, the first passion and the last'
– Samuel Johnson

A few years ago there was a public outcry when Visit Suffolk unveiled a new tourism campaign aimed at luring visitors back to Suffolk. The campaign's slogan was 'The Curious County'. One of Suffolk's MPs branded the slogan 'idiotic and meaningless' and 'a euphemism for something not quite right', and there were calls for the phrase to be dropped. Well, I beg to differ. I think 'The Curious County' sums up Suffolk precisely as well as concisely.

When I was growing up in Suffolk, I knew that the county was special. Our family trips to castles, churches, country houses, farms, woods, forests, beaches, villages and towns alike always offered up something new and fascinating. Suffolk is a county steeped in history, yet still alive and thriving despite the best the Industrial Revolution had to throw at it.

Our Suffolk ancestors left a rich legacy for us to discover and enjoy today. But we must be willing to scratch beneath the surface. And that is what I have tried to do in researching and writing this book. Some of the tales will be familiar to Suffolk die-hards, but hopefully there will be something surprising, funny or odd when you turn the page. I invite you, then, to travel through 'The Curious County' with me, and hope that it is as enjoyable an experience for you as it was for me writing *The A-Z of Curious Suffolk*.

The A–Z of Curious Suffolk

❧ ADULTERY ❧

On 2 April 1828, the *Bury and Norwich Post* reported on the trial and conviction of Thomas Peacock. He was found guilty of bigamous marriages, having been wed to Sarah Steed, spinster, at Lavenham in 1805, to Mary Harnton, spinster, at Elmswell in 1821, and to Mary Green, a widow at Postwick (in Norfolk), in 1824, all of whom were still alive. In passing sentence, the judge said that 'unless I send you out of the country, it is to be feared you will literally make a conquest of all the ladies that come your way'. The judge was clearly not at all impressed with Peacock's crime, adding that: 'Not being content with one or even two wives, your attractions were so irresistible that the last lady (a poor decrepit old woman) was unable to withstand your solicitations, although it was evident she had arrived at that age when no common charms would have been successful.' He further commented that:

> For the preservation, therefore, of the ladies here whose hearts you appear by your fascinating qualifications easily to win, and to prevent the ladies by whom I am surrounded from falling a sacrifice to a person of such agreeable and attractive manners, the sentence of the Court is that you be transported to such place as his Majesty shall direct, for the term of seven years.

Despite the seriousness of the penalty he faced, Thomas Peacock was even heard to comment that he had another two wives in Yorkshire! Thomas was no doubt transported to Australia for the duration of his sentence. Whether or not he ever made it back to Suffolk is not known. But I think it is highly unlikely that he mended his ways and that he continued to leave a trail of wives behind him.

☙❧

In centuries past, it was not just the civil courts who punished those who broke laws. The Church would impose penalties on members of its congregation who transgressed. Either the parish priest himself, or the local church courts, would often require penance to be performed, and such punishments were designed to publicly shame the culprit. Suffolk appears to have its fair share of adulterers and fornicators, and in some cases we have some wonderful detail of both the crime and the punishment. The following account comes from the Ubbeston parish register:

12 Sept 1707 The form of penance to be performed by Sarah Edwards for committing the crime of Adultery as followeth.

Imprimis [firstly] – The said Sarah Edwards shall upon a Sunday after the second Peale of Morning Prayers come out into the Church Porch of Ubbestone and there shall stand until the second lesson be ended arrayed all the while in a white sheet down to the feet with a white wand in her hand and a paper pinned upon her breast expressing her offence and shall ask forgiveness of those that come to church.

An adulterer performing his penance in church.

Item – the second lesson being ended the Minister shall receive her into the Congregation and being placed before the Minister's desk with her face to the Congregation and standing upon a pesse [kneeler] shall make penitently the confession following saying after ye Minister in an audible voice: 'I Sarah Edwards do acknowledge and confess that I have most grievously offended Almighty God and provoked his just wrath and indignation against me by committing the sin of fornication – I am heartily sorry for this my great sin of fornication – I am heartily sorry for this my great sin and offence and I do most sincerely beg of God Almighty pardon and forgiveness thereof and to grant his grace of true repentance and perseverance therein and that I may never commit the like sin anymore but lead an honest and sober life for the time to come …'

No details appear with this account of Sarah's crime, but elsewhere in the register is recorded the baptism of her baby, born out of wedlock. No mention is made of the child's father.

We do know slightly more about the crimes of six individuals punished in Great Welnetham church in 1701. A loose sheet in the parish register tells us that two couples, William and Elizabeth Boldero and Francis and Rose Ottewell, did penance for 'fore antinuptua fornication' which may well imply wife-swapping. Robert Bray and Elizabeth Harold were made to do penance on separate days for fornication with each other. And the following year it was recorded that 'George Cason did his penance for committing fornication with Mary Johnson but shewed no sign of penitence, rather to the contrary'.

⁘ ALE ⁘

Suffolk people are certainly not unusual in their love for alcoholic beverages. Nor is it particularly surprising to learn that in the Middle Ages, church ales were one of England's most traditional and festive forms of ecclesiastical fund-raising. It seems perfectly natural to assume that those people who worshipped together would also drink together. Where Suffolk does stand head and shoulders above many other counties, however, is in the wealth of surviving records and buildings which are testament to this custom.

The surviving parish accounts of Cratfield date back as far as 1490 and tell us that church ales were hosted by Cratfield, or by neighbouring villages, between five and six times a year, raising substantial sums of money. This continued into the early sixteenth century. These festivities were traditionally held on Passion Sunday, Pentecost, All Saints' Day and Plough Monday. Another popular day

The former church house at Fressingfield where ales would have been brewed and sold.
(Tony Scheuregger)

for holding these celebrations was the Fourth Sunday in Lent which is still sometimes called 'Refreshment Sunday'. On these occasions, ales were brewed, yeasty cakes were baked and residents of villages nearby were invited to come and enjoy the day and, of course, buy the food and drink at inflated prices. The visitors didn't mind paying over the odds for their ale and cakes because they knew they could reciprocate on another occasion!

Whilst the majority of the profit from Cratfield's ales appears to have been spent on the church building and ornaments, their church ales were sometimes sold to benefit an individual or a specific cause. Bride ales were sold on behalf of a newly married couple to give them a good financial start in life and help ales were brewed to assist a parishioner who had fallen on bad times.

Fressingfield was one of the fellow parishes who took their turn to produce church ales. In this village, the stunning timber-framed church house, which adjoins the churchyard, still stands. It is sometimes described as the old Guildhall and a beautifully carved wooden corner post depicts St Margaret with whom the guild was said to be associated. Whatever its formal title, it was the place where the church ales would have been brewed and the associated fund-raising events held. It is therefore quite apt that the building is now home to the Fox and Goose Inn.

If you mention the name Jankyn Smith to a resident of Bury St Edmunds, the chances are that there will be some signs of recognition. This may appear remarkable given that he died over 500 years ago, in 1481. But it becomes less surprising when you take into account that he is still commemorated annually in the town. Why? Because he was one of the major benefactors of the community. John Smith (to give him his usual, formal but less memorable name) gave money for the development of St Mary's church, including two new aisles. He also made provision for the enlargement and incorporation of an established college of priests. When Jankyn Smith died he was buried in St Mary's church in the north aisle although his monumental brass above the tomb was later moved to a different part of the church.

More importantly, Jankyn Smith founded a charity originally intended for the payment of town taxes to the abbott of Bury St Edmunds Abbey. But because of the flexibility of the terms under which this charity was set up, it has enabled many generations of townspeople up to the present day to benefit from the money from his endowment. In the seventeenth century, a group of charities of which Jankyn Smith's was the earliest, came to be known as the Guildhall Feoffment. Today, the Guildhall Feoffment runs mainly sheltered housing in three locations in Bury.

Jankyn Smith's will stated that he wanted a requiem mass to be said for his soul in St Mary's church every year on the anniversary of his death (28 June), to be attended by townspeople and residents of almshouses he had established. This 'Commemoration Day', as it has been known since 1662, is still held annually on or very close to 28 June. It is believed to be the oldest, continually held endowed religious service in the world. Smith also stipulated in his will that the residents of his almshouses be given cakes and ale after the service. This tradition is also continued in the eleventh- or twelfth-century Guildhall, where town dignitaries and Guildhall Feoffees assemble with them for a reception to toast their benefactors, surrounded by portraits of these individuals, including one of Jankyn Smith.

⚛

In the nineteenth century, alcohol abuse was a serious problem and the local newspapers are littered with reports of coroners' inquests into deaths due in part or wholly to drink. New laws had been introduced at the beginning of the 1800s which made it easier to open beer-houses in an ordinary home and gin was a particularly cheap liquor. In January 1832 an inquest was held into the death of a

7- year-old boy, Albert Mannell, of Iken, who died from drinking a large quantity of his mother's gin. In June 1841, William Pain, the master of a boat moored at Woodbridge, drowned whilst attempting to board his boat whilst drunk. And in November 1842 the following report appeared in the *Suffolk Chronicle* under the heading 'Caution to Drunkards': 'John Cowey of Rendlesham ... was sent to Woodbridge with Lord Hay's wagon to fetch some deals. He staid there till intoxicated ... Near Wiford Bridge, running alongside the wagon at full trot, he was knocked into a ditch, the wagon overturning upon him.'

Finally this short item from the *Framlingham Weekly News*, reporting on the outcome of the Hartismere Petty Sessions, demonstrates that all sorts of excuses were given to authorities for being intoxicated:

David Storry, Rickinghall, was charged with being drunk and riotous on the highway at Botesdale on 18th April. The case was proved by Inspector Bernard who saw the defendant on the day in question in a beastly state of drunkenness. Defendant pleaded guilty and said he was sorry it had occurred, as he was just upon the point of marrying.

The guilty party was given the option of paying a fine of 10*s* or spending seven days in jail. He chose the former, which perhaps suggests that what was meant by the report was that he was celebrating his impending nuptials on a stag night, rather than getting legless to forget about the forthcoming event.

๑๖๑

If you had asked the average man or woman in a bar in another part of the country at the beginning of the twenty-first century whether they had heard of Aspall Cyder, the answer would probably have been 'no'. However, in just a short space of time the brand has achieved recognition around the world, and it is now unusual not to be able to order a pint of Aspall's in any self-respecting British pub.

Aspall Cyder is by no means a new venture. It was started by Clement Chevalier, who brought cyder making to Suffolk from his native Jersey. Clement had inherited Aspall Hall near Debenham in 1722 from his uncle, Temple Chevalier, but took six years to move into the estate. However, once there it took only a matter of days before he planted his first apple trees, although the local farmers thought he was mad planting on good-quality arable land. The extensive, privately held family archive includes Clement's diaries, accounts and letters which provide a detailed record of his efforts to produce his first

Clement Chevalier (1697–1762) of Aspall Hall.
(Courtesy of Aspall)

cyder in autumn 1728 by buying fruit from local growers. Clement's descendants have been making cyder at the hall ever since. The only female cyder maker in eight generations was Perronelle Guild née Chevallier who took over the running of the business in 1940 on the death of her father. It had been her father, John Barrington Chevalier, who had introduced the 'y' into the name of the drink to differentiate it from the West Country varieties. Perronelle was a founder member of the Soil Association, as a result of which Aspall Cyder became an organic producer; a tradition it maintains to this day. The Cyder House at Aspall Hall, built by Clement Chevalier in 1728, still houses his original mill and horse-drawn press. The heavy granite wheel and trough were brought by ship from France to Ipswich. From there, heavy horses were required to bring them to Aspall, a journey that took three days and which cost £6. When the last press horse died in 1947, the stone wheel and trough were retired and a small petrol-powered dicing machine was installed. The original press is built from wood from the estate and was in continual use until 1971.

⁙ BANG ⁙

Daniel Defoe is best known for his fictitious account of the adventures of shipwrecked Robinson Crusoe on a desert island. But the author was also an active political pamphleteer and, especially in later life, travelled extensively in this country and in Europe. His account of his travels around Britain were first published in the 1720s in three volumes, and his *Tour Through the Eastern Counties* offers an invaluable insight into life in rural Suffolk a few decades before the Industrial Revolution. He would, however, be both complimentary and damning in a few short sentences:

Woodbridge has nothing remarkable, but that it is a considerable market for butter and corn to be exported to London; for now begins that part which is ordinarily called High Suffolk, which, being a rich soil, is for a long tract of ground wholly employed in dairies, and they again famous for the best butter, and perhaps the worst cheese, in England.

Suffolk cheese had a universal reputation for being hard and almost indigestible. It was even known locally as 'bang' or 'thump'. The Suffolk poet Robert Bloomfield said of it, ' … Mocks the weak effort of the bending blade, Or in the hog trough rests in perfect spite, Too big to swallow and too hard to bite'. Although this rather unfair description may have been very accurate, the low quality of the county's cheese was a direct result of the high quality and highly praised butter the same cows produced. After the cream from the milk had been taken to make the butter, it was then further skimmed once or twice. The resulting 'flet' was used to make this coarse cheese.

Nevertheless, Suffolk cheese appeared to have its uses, albeit for a limited time. One commentator wrote, 'The Navy has always issued Suffolk cheese, a thin, hard and durable variety, but practically inedible', and it was because of its long-lasting qualities that it had been chosen by the Admiralty to feed their sailors aboard ship. The diarist Samuel Pepys recorded that he and his wife were 'vexed' at people grumbling about having to eat the product. However, by the 1750s, the Royal Navy had had enough, and condemned it as unfit for their warships, switching to Cheshire and Gloucestershire cheese instead, even though they were probably more expensive and had a shorter shelf life.

❦

Printed in large numbers from the sixteenth to the early twentieth centuries, broadside ballads were the tabloid newspaper of their day. They were printed cheaply on one side of paper and were sold on street corners, in town squares and fairs, and pinned on the walls of alehouses and other public places. They contained song-lyrics, tunes and woodcut illustrations designed to disseminate news, prophecies, histories, moral advice, religious warnings, political arguments, satire, comedy and bawdy tales.

The aftermath of the Gun Cotton Works explosion in August 1871.
(Courtesy of Stowmarket Town Council)

One such broadside ballad, published in 1871, tells of a famous Suffolk tragedy, the first verse of which reads:

> Good people all pray give attention,
> List to what I have to tell,
> Of the sad explosion at Stowmarket,
> That occurred in August, which is known full well.
> Where so many poor souls were injured
> In the height of youth and bloom
> And thro' that sad gun cotton explosion
> Many were cast into an early tomb.

The Stowmarket Gun Cotton Works had been built eight years earlier and provided valuable employment for the townspeople. It manufactured a propellant for gun cartridges and cannon by dipping cotton in a mixture of nitric and sulphuric acid and then washing the fabric. In the afternoon of 11 August 1871 two separate explosions demolished the factory leaving a crater 100ft across and 10ft deep. The noise was heard over 30 miles away, the shock being felt 7 miles away and windows were broken in houses up to 4 miles away from the site. In total twenty-eight people were killed, including two members of the Prentice family who owned the works, and seventy-five more were injured. After the tragedy, an investigation was launched which concluded that the explosion was probably due to a combination of the hot weather and sabotage. Somebody had added acid to the finished gun cotton after it had passed through the testing stage. Nobody was ever caught for the crime. The investigation was the first ever accident to be formally investigated and led to the formation of the world's first Forensic Explosions Laboratory which still exists today. It also led to the introduction of the 1875 Explosions Act.

In February 2014, more than 140 years after the massive, fatal explosion shook the town of Stowmarket, a memorial plaque to those killed in the accident was unveiled in the Old Cemetery. Funded by the Stowmarket Local History Group, the town council and a local funeral director, the plaque was said to be a long overdue monument to the victims because only three of the dead had been buried with headstones. Although a lot of money had been raised to help the affected families in the immediate aftermath of the disaster, the funds were used to repair damaged houses and to support the needy. And so a memorial would not have been contemplated at the time.

☙❧

The now chic seaside resort of Southwold has had a troubled history. Because of its position on the coast, it was vulnerable to attack from the various navies of countries with whom England had grievances over the centuries. Being the nearest coastal point to Holland, Sole Bay, Southwold's coastal waters, was used as an anchorage and watering place for the British fleet during the Dutch Wars. And the considerable merchant and fishing fleet were in constant danger from piracy. Then in 1672 came the Battle of Sole Bay. The English resistance to the Dutch invasion fleet was led by the Duke of York and the Dutch were defeated.

We only know for sure that there were cannon on Gun Hill, pointing out to sea, at the time of the Battle of Sole Bay, although they may have been placed there earlier in the seventeenth century. In 1746 these guns were replaced by the six iron cannon designed to fire 18lb cannonballs. They are said to have been given to the town by the Royal Armouries as a protection to shipping against raids. It is these cannon which stand on Gun Hill today. During the Second World War they were removed and buried so as to avoid giving the Germans any excuse to shell or bomb the town. In fact, the town even offered the guns to the government to be melted down to make newer armaments. There was such an outcry, however, that the cannon stayed put. The last time the guns were fired was in 1842 to celebrate the birthday of the then Prince of Wales.

In July 2015, three of the wooden gun carriages were replaced with new green oak ones made by a boatbuilder in nearby Oulton Broad because the old ones had rotted in the sea air. The other three carriages will hopefully be replaced when a further £12,000 is raised.

☙❧

The last maharajah of the Sikh Empire may have seemed an unlikely person to earn the reputation as the fourth best shot in England. But, at the age of 11, Maharajah Duleep Singh, ruler of the Punjab and owner of the famous Koh-i-noor diamond, was removed from his kingdom by the British East India Company after the Anglo-Sikh Wars and exiled in Britain in 1854. The deposed maharajah became a ward of the British Government and was completely isolated from his family and countrymen. In England he combined the extravagant lifestyle of an Indian prince – redesigning his Suffolk residence Elveden Hall in the style of a Moghul palace – with that of a young English aristocrat. He associated himself with the cream of Victorian society and became a favourite of Queen Victoria who described him as 'extremely handsome … [with] a graceful and dignified manner'.

Duleep Singh had bought Elveden Hall in 1863 and there he indulged his passion for hunting and shooting. He also promoted the little-known method of taking hares by hawking. In 1870, when the war between France and Germany broke out, the entire stud of birds belonging to the Champagne Hawking Club, which had an establishment of some twenty or more hawks (mostly peregrines

Elveden Hall in the 1870s when the Prince of Wales visited to shoot with Maharajah Duleep Singh.

and goshawks), was moved to Elveden Hall. The maharajah sent John Barr, a falconer, to Iceland, to bring back a large stock of falcons.

By the 1870s, Maharajah Duleep Singh was famous for his shooting skills and was among the top shots in the country after the Prince of Wales, who was a regular visitor to Elveden. On his visit in 1876, the future Edward VII wrote, 'We had the most extraordinary good days shooting having killed yesterday and today close on 6000 head, nearly 4500 of which were pheasants! It is certainly the most wonderful shooting I ever saw, and I doubt whether such bags have ever been made before'.

Despite his privileged lifestyle in England, Duleep Singh's movements remained under the strict control of the India Office, a wing of the British Government. He attempted to re-convert to Sikhism, having been converted to Christianity after the fall of his empire. And by the time of his death at the age of 55, he had only been allowed to visit India twice; once to bring his mother to England and three years later to scatter her ashes in their homeland. The maharajah's wish for his body to be returned to India was not honoured. Instead he was buried in Elveden churchyard alongside his first wife and one of their sons.

⁑ BEACONS ⁑

With its long history of maritime trade with other parts of Britain, with the Continent and now increasingly with all corners of the globe, Suffolk has always been aware of the vulnerability of shipping to treacherous waters and sandbanks and to collisions at sea. In 1609, with the backdrop of a spate of losses to shipping along the coal route from Newcastle to London, a petition for seamarks was drawn up by ship-owners and merchants of the east coast who asserted that 'no doubte but everyman that trade with the North partes will willingly contribute thereunto'. This appeal was to Trinity House, a body with an Elizabethan Royal Charter which comprised ships' masters and mariners and which regulated pilotage on the Thames in London. And so the country's first lighthouse was built at Lowestoft.

This first Lowestoft lighthouse comprised a pair of wooden towers illuminated by tallow candles, one high and one low, 'for the direction of ships which crept by night in the dangerous passage betwixt Lowestoft and Winterton'. When these two towers were in line they led ships through the Stanford Channel, an inshore passage which no longer exists. To cover the cost of maintenance and fuel, there was a levy of four pence on every ship passing the light.

In 1676 a new High Lighthouse was built on the cliff at a cost of £300. This was a substantial structure of brick and stone and the light this time was provided by a coal fire, which burned throughout the day as well as at night. None other than Samuel Pepys, the famous diarist, was responsible for this building and a plaque which can still be seen inside the building reads: 'Erected by the brotherhood of Trinity House, Deptford Strond in the Mastership of Samuel Pepys, Esq., Secretary of Ye Admiralty of England A.D. 1676.'

The lighthouse at Lowestoft has seen many more improvements since the seventeenth century. In 1778 oil lamps and reflectors were fitted and just over a century later, in 1874, it was converted to electric lighting. The complement of three lighthouse-keepers that was required at the end of the nineteenth century has since been reduced to just one with the introduction of a fully automated system which can be seen for 20 miles on a clear night. It is one of the most powerful navigation systems in the United Kingdom.

❦

In 1914, the parish church of St James in Bury St Edmunds underwent a dramatic transformation when it became the cathedral church of the newly created Diocese of St Edmundsbury and Ipswich. Up to this point, most churches in Suffolk had come under the pastoral care of the Bishop of Norwich. Unlike many other dioceses in the country, however, the bishop's palace is not in the same town as the cathedral; instead it is in Ipswich. This was, no doubt, a compromise solution to the age-old 'rivalry' between East and West Suffolk. With its historic, religious heritage stretching back many centuries from the

St Edmundsbury Cathedral's Millennium Tower. (Tony Scheuregger)

death and martyrdom of King Edmund, there was a strong argument for the new cathedral to be in Bury St Edmunds. Indeed, the nave of St James' church, which was started in 1503, was the successor to one of the churches within the precincts of the mighty Norman abbey built to house the remains of St Edmund.

The completion and enlargement of St Edmundsbury Cathedral was the inspiration of Stephen Dykes Bower who was the cathedral's architect between 1943 and 1988. He drew up the original design for the completed cathedral, which included a spectacular Gothic tower. Although he was able to see much of his dream become reality – including the rebuilding of the chancel, the creation of transepts and side chapels, and the Song School – there was simply not enough money to complete the tower. When he died in 1994 he left £2 million towards the tower project, which turned into what became the ambitious Millennium Project. Some £4 million was raised from a public appeal to which the Millennium Commission added £6 million in matching funding. Prince Charles, the Prince of Wales, was the project's patron and laid the first brick in July 2001. In an earlier comment about the scheme he called the new tower a 'spiritual beacon of the future'. Unfortunately the *East Anglian Daily Times* misprinted the quote, leading to comment in the national press about pigs flying (they had printed it as 'spiritual bacon').

The completion of the splendid new cathedral tower, made from English limestone clad with Barnack and Clipsham stone, was marked with a celebratory service on 22 July 2005 which was attended by the Prince of Wales and the Duchess of Cornwall. It was, however, another five years before the new tower was 'crowned' with a magnificent vaulted ceiling which won the Royal Institute of Architects East 'Spirit of Ingenuity' Award 2010.

᠙

Horseracing has long been known as the 'Sport of Kings' and it is certainly true that the fortunes of a little Suffolk market town, surrounded by rolling heathland, were changed forever when King James I decided to pursue two of his favourite pastimes, hunting and hawking. He therefore established himself in Newmarket in 1605. King James' son and grandson – Charles I and Charles II – were both good riders and horseracing flourished in the town. It was Charles II who did more than any other monarch to advance the sport of horseracing in Britain and he instituted, by Act of Parliament in 1665, the first race to be run in Britain under written rules.

The earliest racecourse in Newmarket was the Long Course which was over 8 miles long and the first recorded horserace was in 1613 when the 'scarcity of lodgings in the town compelled many courtiers to stay at Linton near the other end of the course'. Over time, 4 miles became the most popular race distance and the Beacon Course became the main Newmarket racecourse; the name is first found in 1680. Many paintings of the Newmarket races of the eighteenth century depict the Beacon Course. The Beacon Post is one of the highlights of a tour of the National Horseracing Museum in the town. This starting post is a square wooden post and represents the many posts which would have been dotted around Newmarket Heath from the seventeenth century onwards, marking the starts and finishes of the course as well as the turning points and the places where to lay a bet. A second surviving post in the museum is the Red Post, which was a betting post near the end of the Beacon Course. Parts of the Beacon Course are still in use today.

⚜ CLERICS ⚜

Parish priests have been the mainstay of rural communities across the country for centuries. As you might expect, some have been good and some bad. But Suffolk can boast a bogus cleric who caused an Act of Parliament to be drawn up.

George Wilfred Frederick Ellis was appointed as curate at Wetheringsett in 1883 and the following year was instituted as rector of the parish. He was a conscientious clergyman and performed many baptisms, marriages and burial services for villagers. Almost five years later, Ellis was found out to be a fraud. He had apparently forged documents which stated that he had been ordained into the Roman Catholic Church. Armed with these, he had duped senior churchmen into believing that he had converted to the Church of England and had subsequently acquired a clerical position.

Ellis' trial in March 1888 at the Eye Petty Sessions and then at the Bury St Edmunds Assizes elicited widespread coverage in both the local and national press; the *Ipswich Journal* devoted over a whole page to the case. He was charged that he 'knowingly, wilfully and feloniously pretending to be in holy orders, did solemnise matrimony according to the rites of the Church of England in the parish church of Wetheringsett'. During his trial it emerged that he was, in fact, a humble tailor from Lincolnshire who had probably hit upon the deception whilst acting as usher in the Roman Catholic College in Salford. The Bishop of Norwich and several other important clergymen were called as witnesses after which time the jury took only five minutes to return a guilty verdict. Ellis was sentenced to seven years' penal servitude which he served in Dartmoor Prison.

The scene of the 'Akenham Burial Scandal' in 1878. (Tony Scheuregger)

However, George Ellis' trial was not the end of the story. The uneasy residents of Wetheringsett, especially those who had been married by the bogus cleric, wondered what the status of these unions were and that of any children they had had after marriage. As a result, the Marriages Validation Act 1888 was passed which recognised all of the marriages Ellis had performed 'as valid as if the same had been solemnised before a duly ordained clergyman of the Church of England'.

⚮

The now redundant Akenham church near Ipswich is surrounded, as you might expect, by a churchyard with gravestones in varying states of decay and neglect. But in this one is a memorial to Joseph Ramsey, who died in 1878 aged 2 years. His burial led to a legal trial which resulted in a change in funeral practices as set out in the Burial Law Amendment Act 1880.

Shortly before 5 p.m. on Friday, 23 August 1878, the rector, the Revd George Drury, set out to bury 2-year-old Joseph Ramsey. He had been told that the boy's parents were Baptists, and that their son was therefore unbaptised (because Baptists practise adult baptism). This meant that Drury was unable to read the Book of Common Prayer burial service over the coffin. But the boy could certainly be buried in consecrated ground, in this case in the north side of the churchyard where unbaptised infants were traditionally laid to rest.

It is not clear what actually took place at the church that day. But what is known for certain is that the little coffin arrived accompanied by a Congregationalist minister, the Revd Wickham Tozer, and a crowd of between twenty or thirty farm labourers who were colleagues of the dead boy's father. Most of these people, too, were members of various Ipswich Nonconformist churches. The Revd Tozer then started to hold a funeral service at the edge of a field a little way from the churchyard gate. The Revd Drury apparently then tried to take charge of the coffin and take it to the prepared grave in the churchyard, but a 'fight' ensued between the two clergymen resulting in Drury storming off and locking the churchyard gate. The assembled crowd and remaining cleric therefore carried the coffin through the hedge into the churchyard and buried it. The crucial legal point raised was whether or not the Revd Tozer had read a burial service over the coffin whilst in the churchyard. If so, this would have been a crime under legislation which prohibited clergymen of any other denomination reading a burial service in a Church of England churchyard. The Revd Tozer and witnesses claimed that this did not take place inside the churchyard but in the field before the coffin was moved.

The resulting court case to resolve this dispute received national coverage under the heading 'The Akenham Burial Scandal'. There was also widespread public criticism in the form of letters to the newspapers, especially criticising the Revd Drury's draconian approach. By coincidence, a new bill on burial reform was before Parliament and the Akenham case certainly influenced the debates in both Houses. The resulting Act of Parliament two years later therefore altered the burial provisions and meant that Nonconformist burial services were allowed in Church of England churchyards.

⊙�⊙

Suffolk appears to have had more than its fair share of ecclesiastical troubles. In the 1870s, the otherwise peaceful parish of Little Stonham erupted into a spate of arguments between clerics and their congregation as well as a war between two clergymen.

The first part of this saga involved two main protagonists. The first was the Revd William Barlee who had been appointed curate at the parish church in 1870. The second character was Edgar Harvey, an ordinary farm labourer who was an enthusiastic worshipper and, more important, a person who liked to sing. The trouble was that the curate's wife, who believed herself knowledgeable in musical matters, thought that Harvey's voice was 'uncultivated' and that it had no place in church. Harvey and his small band of fellow singers were banished from the singing gallery and replaced by a children's choir. The relationship between the Barlees and the church organist (who was on their side), and Edgar Harvey became more and more acrimonious until the Revd Barlee decided that the best way to deal with the situation was to ban singing in Little Stonham church altogether; the services were to be said from then on. The situation finally came to a head in October 1873 when, during the Sunday afternoon service when the Revd Barlee had started to read the *Magnificat*, Harvey and four of his friends started singing. The curate commanded them to stop – which they didn't. And so he ordered the local constable to eject the men from the church. A court case brought against Edgar Harvey at which Barlee accused him of 'disturbing and disquieting the congregation assembled by singing aloud' lasted six hours despite its trivial nature. The newspaper report in the *Ipswich Journal* points to much hilarity in court, not least when Mr Harvey's solicitor described Little Stonham as a place where his client's singing was infinitely more entertaining than sitting through a William Barlee sermon! Edgar Harvey was found not guilty, which was received with loud applause from the assembled crowd. From then on the Revd Barlee was clearly not a popular man in the neighbourhood and the newspapers reported the following January that the curate was bound over to keep the peace over an incident where he bad-mouthed one of Edgar Harvey's friends who no longer attended church services.

And so what of the the Revd Barlee's boss, the rector? Enter, then, the third protagonist. In September 1877 the *Bury and Norwich Post* reported on a case brought before the Needham Market Petty Sessions against the rector, the Revd Richard Askew, for being drunk and riotous. It told readers that some unpleasant feeling had existed between the defendant and his curate, the Revd Barlee, and that when the rector was the worse for drink he had called Barlee 'a ——— blackguard' and 'a ——— Cambridge snob' amongst other things. He had also tried to hit the curate but was restrained by a policeman. The magistrates fined him 40*s* with costs and bound him over to keep the peace for six months. The Revd Askew was later suspended from his parish for a year for a similar offence. The Revd Barlee moved on fairly soon afterwards to a parish in Norfolk.

☙❦

It is not often that an argument between two clerics ends in murder. But in 1887 in the village of Cretingham this is exactly what happened. The *East Anglian Daily Times* summed up the story after a criminal trial with 'Vicar of

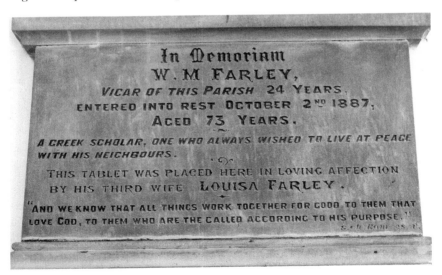

The Revd Farley's memorial in Cretingham church. (Tony Scheuregger)

Cretingham murdered by his curate'. But this horrific crime was not a result of a minor disagreement over church services or communion wine. And so all the gory details were picked up by the national press as well as publications such as the *Illustrated Police News* which featured on its front page sketches of the main characters as well as imaginings of the scene of crime and the trial.

In short, the rather elderly Revd William Meymott Farley died a horrible death in the middle of the night in his own bedroom after having been slashed from ear to ear with a cut-throat razor. His curate, the Revd Arthur Gilbert-Cooper, who had a history of mental illness and violence, was convicted of the crime. The initial verdict, delivered by a jury at a coroner's inquest held at the Bell Inn in Cretingham, followed the following summing up by the coroner:

> I don't think I shall detain you very long in this case. The most material evidence is that of Mrs Farley. It seems that the prisoner was seen by Mrs Farley to go into the room of the deceased with a candle in one hand, and she knows not what in the other. He had been there but a short time when the deceased appears to have called out that his throat was cut. Whether that statement was made in the hearing of the prisoner or not Mrs Farley cannot possibly say, but at any rate the deceased's throat was cut, and a razor was found in the prisoner's bedroom under the looking glass, hid up, apparently with blood on it. A small quantity of blood was also seen on his clothes.

Gilbert-Cooper was declared insane and therefore avoided the hangman's noose. Instead he was sent to the secure asylum at Broadmoor under the then relatively recent Criminal Lunacy Act 1884 where he spent the rest of his life.

But the case may not have been as cut and dried as it seemed. Local rumours suggested that the curate, who also lived in the house, was having an affair with the Revd Farley's wife – clearly a strong motive for murder. Mrs Harriet Louisa Farley was much younger than her husband although older than the guilty man. And shortly after the murder, Mrs Farley simply disappeared with the £900 she inherited from her late husband. It now transpires that she had a rocky relationship with her first husband before she met the Revd Farley. This husband, too, had been considerably older than her. Had Mrs Farley murdered her vicar husband in frustration over his advancing years, being keen to move on to a younger husband? To date, nobody has uncovered the truth about Harriet Louisa Farley and so the case remains firmly closed, done and dusted.

❧ CRANKLE ❧

It is widely accepted that Suffolk has more 'crinkle crankle' walls (more than fifty) than all the other counties in England put together. Indeed, the village of Easton is said to have the longest surviving example in the world of this type of wall. In fact, even the term 'crinkle crankle' is said to be derived from the Suffolk dialect and is an Old English term for zig-zag. These constructions are sometimes known as serpentine, ribbon or wavy walls elsewhere, but any self-respecting East Anglian will refer to them as 'crinkle crankle'. We probably owe their existence, though, to Dutch engineers who came over to the region in the seventeenth century to help drain the Fens.

A crinkle crankle wall is an ingenious design. It economises on bricks because it can be built just one brick thick. Unlike straight walls, which need multiple thicknesses of bricks or buttresses to provide stability, a wavy wall provides its own reinforcement. And the purpose of such walls is equally clever. They are most frequently to be found bordering a garden or an orchard and are aligned east–west so that one side faces south. The curves in the wall traps the sun's rays, warming up the garden and creating a micro-climate. Thus, this helped the growing of fruit, in particular more exotic varieties like peaches and figs.

Bury St Edmunds boasts two rivers, the Linnet and the Lark, as well as 150 acres of meadows and natural riverbanks, all in the centre of the town. And the land surrounding the two rivers has played an essential role for residents for centuries. The three water meadows, dating back to the twelfth century, provided natural protection for the medieval town as well as helping to alleviate flooding at various times in Bury's history.

The Crankles is a triangular piece of land between the two rivers just before they meet in what is now the Abbey Gardens. Until the Dissolution of the Monasteries by Henry VIII, the abbey in Bury St Edmunds was one of the most powerful in the country. It dominated the town and owned great swathes of land. The Crankles were originally the abbey's fishponds and lay next to the 12-acre vineyard which was first planted by the monks in the thirteenth century. The fishponds, created from diverted water from the Linnet and the Lark with their abundant fish, provided much-needed food for the monastic community.

Until early 2015, Cricket Bat Willow (*Salix alba coerulea*) covered the Crankles. They had first been grown there in 1780 because the land had very

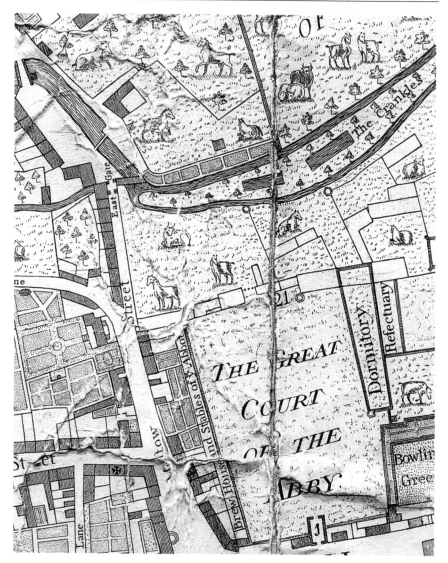

The Crankles, the former fishponds of Bury St Edmunds Abbey, shown on a 1776 map.
(Courtesy of Dr Pat Murrell. Photographer: Tony Scheuregger)

damp soil. The tree's lightweight, strong timber is the only wood from which decent cricket bats can be made. The willows were felled by a specialist cricket bat maker to be cut into 28in lengths, cleft and sawn into the rough shapes of blades, waxed and air dried for several months before the final processing into finished bats. In accordance with the felling licence, the Crankles will, sadly, not be replanted with Cricket Bat Willow but will be restocked with fruit and native hardwood species to encourage pollinating insects.

❧ DISEASE ❧

When Dr Jane Walker, one of Britain's earliest female medical pioneers, was looking for a suitable site on which to build a sanatorium for the treatment of patients with tuberculosis, she had a number of criteria the place had to fulfil. These included cold, fresh air, and a south-facing situation preferably on sandy soil where pine trees would grow. Dr Walker had opened a similar centre in Downham Market, Norfolk, in 1896 and was now looking for a second site. She found the ideal spot in Nayland and Wissington, Suffolk, and in 1901 the East Anglian Sanatorium was opened.

Dr Walker had studied the handling of tuberculosis sufferers in Germany, which consisted of rest, good food, plenty of fresh air and a carefully controlled exercise regime. A cure for the disease was still some way off but the open-air method appeared to put patients into remission, allowing them to return to their normal lives. And so at her sanatorium in Suffolk Dr Walker followed this treatment pattern. She was, however, said to have some rather eccentric ideas, such as insisting that the children wore no shoes, even in the depths of winter.

The first building to be erected in Nayland was a private hospital but this was followed by two more sanatoria in 1904 and 1912, the latter of which was for children. These two new institutions were, at first, supported by the income from the original sanatorium, although both central and local government also contributed funding from 1912 onwards. The combined site dominated the life of the two villages of Nayland and Wissington between the two wars.

An early advertising postcard for the East Anglian Sanatorium.
(Courtesy of the Nayland with Wissington Conservation Society)

The local inn served medical practitioners and visitors alike and the local householders provided accommodation for the sanatoria's staff and patients' families when visiting.

Dr Walker died in 1938 and without her driving energy the East Anglian Sanatorium fell into financial difficulties. It was first taken on by the local authority and then by the British Legion in 1943. It finally closed in 1959 when all such establishments closed following the discovery of streptomycin, a cure for tuberculosis. The main building became the Jane Walker Hospital for those with learning disabilities and the others became four private houses.

❦

In the seventeenth century Needham Market on the River Gipping was a prosperous town due to its buoyant wool-combing industry, supporting the other weaving towns in Suffolk. However, its fortunes were reversed almost overnight in 1663 when plague swept through the town causing it to be isolated for two years from the surrounding area. Its trade was lost and the community never returned to the same line of work.

During this isolation, a chain was erected at both ends of the parish which clearly acted not so much as a physical barrier but as a psychological deterrent. Chainbridge in the west of the town, and Chainhouse Road and Chain House Farm to the east, are present-day reminders of the points at which the townspeople would leave money in return for food which was left by residents outside the exclusion zone. The residents' coins were soaked in vinegar as it was thought that this sterilised the infection.

Although sadly no detailed records exist of the effect of the plague on Needham Market, it was said that the town became so rundown that grass grew in the streets and that the dead were buried in fields near to the Chainbridge. It is also possible that the earlier victims who died of the plague were taken down the street known today as The Causeway to nearby Barking church for burial: this name is thought to be a corruption of 'The Corpseway'. There were so-called 'sick houses' near the river, and on higher ground were 'airing houses' where those few residents unaffected by the disease would live.

Luckily some townspeople did survive and in 1665 the community was declared plague-free. Due in part to better policing of ships entering the ports of East Anglia, this was the last serious outbreak of the plague in Suffolk.

❦

Smallpox was a disease which ravaged the country in the eighteenth and early nineteenth centuries. Even after vaccines were discovered and became available, outbreaks still occurred with some frequency and rapidity, affecting the sufferers (an average of one in three died in the 1700s) and having a devastating impact on local businesses. The causes of the disease were still misunderstood and so local authorities were often blamed for allowing poorer housing to become overcrowded and rundown with poor sanitation.

Because of its position on the coast and being a major port, Lowestoft was always more vulnerable than inland towns to epidemics. In 1871 the authorities were instructed by the government to inspect all vessels arriving from a place infected with cholera, which was the current threat to public health. One of the doctors who went aboard these vessels, J.S. Worthington, suggested that the town might have a floating hospital to deal with cholera victims arriving from overseas, instead of bringing them and their disease onto dry land. The Lowestoft Improvement Commissioners therefore bought a wherry and kitted it out with a large room with five beds, another with three beds and facilities for the medical staff. The fit-out cost £151 4s.

Luckily for the residents of Lowestoft the feared cholera outbreak of 1871 did not materialise. However, smallpox did. For two years a smallpox epidemic raged through Western Europe and in 1872 it reached Lowestoft. In January seventy-five cases had been recorded with forty-five infected houses and the floating hospital clearly had not enough capacity. And so plans were drawn up for an isolation hospital and the building was erected in just two weeks. It offered beds for up to thirty people, both private and pauper patients, supported by an increase in the town's rates. Although the hospital had a few administrative problems, it and the floating hospital coped with the smallpox outbreak competently and in August 1872 the town was declared free of the disease.

In a report in January 1874, the Medical Officer of Health in the Port of London said that Lowestoft's floating hospital was highly satisfactory. The town had been the first port to build such a vessel and it was equal to any of the others subsequently constructed elsewhere. Sadly it did not survive very much longer: repairs on the hull were not kept up and the boat sunk in its moorings.

☙❧

A visitor to Helmingham church cannot fail to notice the rather magnificent, oversized memorial to four generations of the Tollemache family, the Lords of the Manor of Helmingham since the late fifteenth century. Other memorials adorn

Lady Catherine Tollemache's memorial in Helmingham church. (Tony Scheuregger)

almost every available wall space. By comparison, one rather understated black marble plaque on the south wall of the chancel is to a rather remarkable female member of the Tollemache clan. She was Catherine, wife of Lionel Tollemache, who died in 1620. The inscription includes the following lines: 'while she lived for her pietie towards God, pitie towards the poore, & charitie in releeving (through her skill & singular experience in chyrurgerie [surgery]), the sick & sore wounded, was beloved & honoured of all, as now missed & lamented in her death'.

All Elizabethan and Jacobean women of Catherine's standing were expected to be well-educated, devoting time to pursuits allied to their primary responsibility for hospitality and running of the household. But a woman's involvement in surgery was probably undertaken rather more discreetly both inside and outside of the family home. At this time professional practice was strictly the preserve of men and there was a clear demarcation between physicians, who dealt with medical disorders, and barber-surgeons who dealt with wounds and other treatments requiring a sharp blade. Catherine's memorial inscription, however, suggests that she was active in both fields of medicine and the survival of a collection of Catherine Tollemache's books and manuscripts in Helmingham Hall (which is still the Tollemache ancestral home today) also bears witness to this.

Among Catherine's library, inscribed by her in the front, is a collection of seventeen sets of advice, four of which are written by Catherine herself. Instructions for creating sweets sit alongside those for preserving green apples and a cure for the plague. Among Catherine Tollemache's own contributions is the method by which flesh might be removed from a bone. It reads:

> To escalle a bone: Take one dramme of mere [myrrh] and the water of snalles [snails] the water of scantem [?] and aquafire [aqua vitae] toe or thre dropes; and wete lent [wet lint] and laye upon the bone and ete away the flesh and with burnt allume [burnt alum] marcurie presipetat [mercury precipitate] and a very litell white marcurie [white mercury] this must be laid under wher the bone ise not bare.

In the late 1500s, understanding of infection was limited and so procedures of this kind would demand close skills of observation and prompt action if necessary. Myrrh and various snail products were commonly found in remedies at this time. Myrrh, in particular, had been used in Chinese medicine from ancient times and its applications included treatment of impact injury, incised wounds and hard to heal bones. If Catherine Tollemache did use this and other procedures she recorded in her own hand – and there is clear evidence to suggest this was the case – she was a truly outstanding woman and deserving of such a glowing tribute as on her memorial.

❧ DOGS ❧

Most parts of Britain have their own version of the black dog legend. And each region has a different name for the beast, for example Northern England has Padfoot, Shriker or Trash, and Wales has the Gwyllgi. But probably the most unforgettable black dog case dates back to 4 August 1577 when 'a Straunge and terrible Wunder' befell the churches of St Mary's Bungay and Blythburgh.

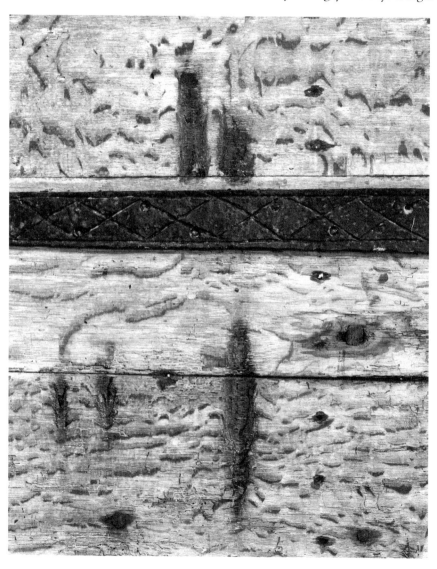

The marks on the north door in Blythburgh church said to have been made by the Black Shuck in 1577. (Tony Scheuregger)

During morning service in Bungay, an unusually violent storm was raging outside when the proceedings were disrupted by a huge black dog which burst in surrounded by lightning flashes. It swept through the building 'with greate swiftnesse and incredible haste among the people' and when it passed between two of the worshippers it 'wrung the necks of them bothe at one instant clene backward insomuch that, even at moment where they kneeled, they straungely died.' Another unfortunate man survived but was shrivelled up 'like a piece of leather scorched in a hot fire'.

This dog, known locally as Black Shuck (from the Danish *succa* to mean the Devil or evil spirits), was believed by the witnesses to this event to have been the Devil in animal form. As well as its fearsome appearance, it was reported to have had a sulphurous smell, and when the places where it had been were examined there was a smell of brimstone as well as the ground being scorched.

We know so much detail about this canine visitation because of a contemporary pamphlet written and published by the Revd Abraham Fleming, a prolific author on all sorts of subjects from earthquakes to translations of Latin classics. In *A Straunge and terrible Wunder* Fleming also tells how, on the very same day, the Black Shuck appears some 10 miles away in Blythburgh accompanied again with a flash of lightning which struck the spire sending tons of masonry through the roof, and killing two men and a young lad. The dog also left his trademark in the form of deep, black claw marks, on the north door of the church (which can still be seen today).

There have been many sightings of the Black Shuck in the North East and along the coast of Suffolk since the sixteenth century. Not all of the dogs appear to cause destruction and death. In Leiston, for example, the Galleytrot (another Suffolk name for the beast) has been seen on the stroke of midnight slinking around among the tombstones in the churchyard 'like an evil whisper'. The name Galleytrot is thought to be a corruption of '*Gardez le Tresor!*' or 'Guard the Treasure' and probably comes from the story of St Felix having buried his treasure at Clopton Hall near Great Bealings, guarded by a huge dog and a monk. So the vicinity is said to be haunted by an enormous hound with a monk's head.

⧉

Nowadays we can train 'Man's best friend' to do almost anything. But the following story, printed in the *Bury and Norwich Post* of 4 September 1822, seems quite a remarkable feat:

Mr John Freeman of Framsden, some time since, gave to Mr Chas. Freeman of Stowupland, a mastiff bitch (and her whelp) which is now kept by him, and which regularly goes twice a week, sometimes thrice, from Stowupland to the parish of Framsden (in the night), thereby establishing a post between the two parties, being a distance of about nine miles. Letters are secured upon the dog's neck in the evening, by Mr Freeman of Stowupland and are received by Mr Freeman of Framsden the following morning; the dog remains during the day, never longer, and returns to Stowupland, where letters are received the succeeding morning.

This was certainly an ingenious way to circumvent the postal system at the time which was in some disarray and rife with corruption. I wonder whether they continued to use their personal communication system after reform of the British postal system and the invention of the Penny Black stamp in 1840?

⸭ EDUCATION ⸭

This county is not unusual in that its villages and towns played host to simply thousands of so-called dame schools which reached their peak in the first half of the nineteenth century. Suffolk at this time, however, was suffering from a particular lack of education for working-class children. Dame schools were private, local initiatives, each run by one woman in her home, aimed at providing a basic education to children from the labouring classes. What is more uncommon, however, is that we have some fascinating, surviving first-hand accounts of the women who ran these schools in the village of Wortham. That said, they are rather biased comments.

The Revd Richard Cobbold was the Rector of Wortham from 1824 until his death in 1877. Aside from his spiritual and pastoral duties, he was a prolific writer. By far his most successful book was *The History of Margaret Catchpole: A Suffolk Girl* which brought him national and international recognition. His more interesting (unpublished) work, however, was the various volumes of notes and observations, together with his own watercolour illustrations, of the goings-on in Wortham focussed on the characters of the various residents. On his arrival in the village, the Revd Cobbold set up a Sunday school and then in the 1840s a day school for some ninety boys and girls. He was therefore quite scathing in this comments about the illiteracy of the women who ran the dame schools: characters like Rebecca Bobby and Maria Jolly who he wrote about in his account of Wortham 'notables'.

The original entrance to Wortham School established by the Revd Richard Cobbold in the 1840s.
(Tony Scheuregger)

According to the Revd Cobbold, Rebecca Bobby 'did more with her eye than with her book of instruction'. She was an extremely neat and clean person who exacted the same standards from everyone who entered her house. She taught the alphabet and how to thread a needle. Cobbold derides Mrs Bobby by saying that her scholars were as learned as herself, the dame being very ignorant and, like many who taught young children, was imposing rather than enlightening.

Maria Jolly was described at her marriage as a schoolmistress and so brought her desire to educate poorer children to Wortham from her home in Wetheringsett. Cobbold described Mrs Jolly as a very bad reader and a still worse writer, although one with an inflated sense of her own importance. The rector describes how the letters she wrote needed much deciphering. According to Cobbold, all Mrs Jolly's advice was contained in just one phrase, 'Be a good girl (or boy)'.

Summerhill is a real place, not a utopia. Living in a community of around 100 people is not always easy. Everybody is learning about themselves, and on a bleak January day, with the east wind blowing, things are sometimes not wonderful! But Summerhill in summertime is lush, green and not unlike never-never land. It is more a family or tribe than a school – full of companionship, laughter and real feelings. For many Summerhill pupils, it becomes the most meaningful experience in their lives.

This is how only the third principal in this school's existence describes the world-famous, co-educational boarding school. It has been on the same premises near Leiston since 1927 after six years of moves from a suburb of Dresden, Germany, to Sonntagsberg in Austria and then to the Dorset town of Lyme Regis.

Summerhill was the creation of Alexander Sutherland Neill and runs according to his guiding principle 'Freedom, not Licence'. It is arranged as a democratic community where all aspects of school life are decided by pupils and teachers alike, all of whom have an equal vote at meetings. They are free to do as they choose as long as their actions do not cause harm to others. The important freedom at Summerhill is the right to play. All lessons are optional. There is no pressure to conform to adult ideas of growing up, although the community itself has expectations of reasonable conduct from all individuals. Bullying, vandalism or other anti-social behaviour is dealt with by specially elected ombudsmen, or can be brought to the whole community in its regular meetings. After Neill's death in 1973, the school was run by his widow Ena and then by his daughter who is the current principal.

The school became renowned through A.S. Neill's writings and lectures, and many 'copycat', democratic schools have sprung up, especially in the United States. He is recognised as being amongst the top twelve men and women who influenced British schooling in the last millennium. As might be expected, Summerhill has had a difficult relationship with the British Government, which regulates and maintains standards of education for all children in the country. This came to a peak in the 1990s when the school was issued with a notice of complaint centered on the school's policy of non-compulsory lessons. After a high-profile court case in 2000, a compromise settlement was reached. The school continues to operate with some seventy-five pupils aged between 5 and 17.

⚛

François de la Rochefoucauld and his brother stayed for a year in Bury St Edmunds in 1784; a time when the town was considered at the height of its prosperity and a fashionable place to be and to be seen. The 18-year-old Frenchman toured the region and recorded his observations of life, in particular in Suffolk. He wrote about almost everything from travel to the English climate in a diary he wrote for his father back in France. His rather amusing and critical account of English culture is summed up in this passage based on his observations at public balls:

> Dancing plays the smallest part in the pleasures of the English – in general, they have no taste for this amusement … The two sexes dance equally badly, without the least grace, no steps, no rhythm … The women hold themselves badly, the head hanging forward, the arms dangling, the eyes lowered … the men with their knees bent; they suddenly change direction with their legs; in short their appearance is most disagreeable as they dance.

Something the Frenchman does not comment on, however, is the considerable effort the middle and upper classes appear to have taken to try to educate their offspring in such refinements as dancing and music. But then he may well have been incredulous at the amount of money spent on such specialist teaching if he did not appreciate the results!

The eighteenth-century local newspapers are simply littered with advertisements for privately run academies for young ladies and for young men. One such typical example, published in the *Ipswich Journal* of 19 June 1742, gives details of a boarding school for young ladies in St Clement's Street, Ipswich, run by John and Harriet Wood. While Mrs Wood taught needlework and English, she paid for visiting masters to educate her charges in writing and arithmetic. Her husband was the music and dancing master:

… For Learning to Dance, half a Guinea Entrance, and fifteen Shillings per Quarter, and at a Ball five Shillings … For Learning on the Spinnet [a keyboard instrument], half a Guinea Entrance, and fifteen Shillings a Quarter, and half a Crown per Quarter more for the Use of an Instrument, and keeping it in order.

The title page of the first edition of John Playford's *The English Dancing Master*.

Mr Wood also taught dancing as a visiting master at a number of other similar schools in the area. No doubt he would have used as his 'bible' *The English Dancing Master*, a highly successful manual published in several editions by John Playford and his successors. It contained the music and instructions on the relevant steps for over one hundred English country dances.

⚘ EXCURSIONS ⚘

> I set out, the 3d of April, 1722, going first eastward, and took what I think, I may very honestly call a circuit in the very letter of it; for I went down by the coast of the Thames thro' the marshes or hundreds, on the south-side of the county of Essex, till I came to Malden, Colchester, and Harwich, thence continuing on the coast of Suffolk to Yarmouth; thence round by the edge of the sea, on the north and west-side of Norfolk, to Lynn, Wisbich [sic], and the Wash; thence back again on the north-side of Suffolk and Essex, to the west, ending it in Middlesex, near the place where I began it, reserving the middle or centre of the several counties to some little excursions, which I made by themselves.

And so, Daniel Defoe set out on his tour of the Eastern Counties. There had been other travel writers before the eighteenth century, most notably William Camden who, in 1586, published *Britannia*, the first known geographical and historical survey of Great Britain and Ireland. And in the late seventeenth century, Celia Fiennes famously wrote an account of her travels *Through England on a Side Saddle*. Whilst Camden's account is purely factual, focussing on the great houses and the landed gentry, Celia Fiennes comments to a limited degree on what she sees and does. Defoe, however, attempts to educate the reader, not holding back in voicing his own opinion on what he sees in Suffolk on his excursions. For example, after touring the Suffolk coast he wrote:

> I find very little remarkable on this side of Suffolk, but what is on the sea shore … the inland country is that which they properly call High-Suffolk, and is full of rich feeding-grounds and large farms, mostly employ'd in dayries for making the Suffolk butter and cheese … Among these rich grounds stand some market-towns, tho' not of very considerable note; such as Framlingham …

Many might be surprised at his views on Framlingham, a rather fine market town with its historic castle and church.

Framlingham, a market town 'not of very considerable note' according to Daniel Defoe.
(Tony Scheuregger)

Luckily, a decade or so later, the balance was redressed in what might be considered the first guidebook for visitors to Suffolk. In 1735, John Kirby published his 'roadbook', *The Suffolk Traveller.* The subtitle he gives it explains the purpose: *A journey through Suffolk in which is inserted the true distance in the roads, from Ipswich to every market town in Suffolk, the same from Bury St Edmunds. Likewise the distance in the roads from one village to another; with notes of direction for travellers, as what churches and gentlemen's seats are passed by, and on which side of the road, and the distance they are at from either of the said towns. With a short historical account of the antiquities of every market town, monasteries, castles etc that were in former times.* This book gave visitors to Suffolk a concise description of all the main towns and villages, offering useful information such as the market days and fairs taking place. Although mainly factual, Kirby allows his own views to creep in, in order to guide the user. This is how Kirby starts his description of the same town:

> Framlingham is a parish of large extent, in the midst of which standeth the church and market. The town is pleasantly seated, and pretty well built, upon a clay hill near the head of the River Ore; which rising in the hills on the north passeth through the town and falleth into the sea beyond Orford. The market is weekly, on Saturday; and there is a fair on Monday and Tuesday in Whitson-Week … and another fair on Michaelmas-Day.

This publication, therefore, can be seen as the forerunner to the plethora of visitors' guides to the county produced right up to the present day.

⚜ FIRE ⚜

We know that many of the large towns, as well as the villages, in Suffolk have suffered several devastating fires in their history. In April 1608, a conflagration in Bury St Edmunds consumed 160 houses plus many other buildings with damages totalling £60,000. And in June 1667 a 'great fire' destroyed almost all of Haverhill. Before the introduction of fire insurance, the main way in which a community might raise the huge sums of money required for rebuilding was to apply to the monarch, requesting them to authorise the issue of an appeal for donations. Consent to make the appeal was authorised by the Crown in a Letters Patent. The appeal would be read out in churches within a particular county or area. The Book of Common Prayer of 1662 gave instructions when in the service the brief was to be read, and the churchwardens would then take the collection. 'Please remember the brief' would be their cry. House-to-house collections in the parish would also be carried out if authorised in the brief.

One such town which successfully petitioned for the issue of a brief was Bungay, following a fire which had broken out just before sunrise on 1 March 1688 in a small, uninhabited tenement. The brief picks up the story of the fire:

> … which spread itself so irresistibly, that in four hours the flames consumed the whole town except one small street and a few houses; and destroyed one of the churches, being a large and magnificent building, together with a free-school, and three alms-houses; two eminent market crosses, and the dwelling-houses of one hundred and ninety families; many brewing offices, shops, warehouses, barns, and other houses, near four hundred in number; in which most of the sufferers, through the sudden and violent rage of the flames, lost all their house hold-stuff, stock, goods, and substance: the loss amounting to £29,898, and upwards.

Woodcut from *A brief sonnet declaring the lamentation of Beckles, a Market Town in Suffolk* which describes a great fire of 1586.

Some members of the church congregations wearied over the number of briefs being issued, and the amount of money they were asked to contribute to affected communities they hadn't even heard of, let alone visited. Samuel Pepys wrote in his famous diary, 'To church, where we observe the trade of briefs is come now up to so constant a course every Sunday, that we resolve to give no more to them.' However, the practice continued until 1828 when it was eventually abolished due to a combination of factors including abuse of the system, administrative costs and, thankfully, the wide availability of insurance against such acts of God.

☙

The parish of St Clement's in Ipswich was the backdrop for an extraordinary event which was recorded in the world's first scientific journal, begun in 1662, the *Philosophical Transactions of the Royal Society of London*. In it, a Dr Lobb reports on two separate but similar accounts from clergymen in Ipswich who spoke to eyewitnesses.

The periodical says:

> One Grace Pett, a fisherman's wife, aged about 60, had a custom for several years past, of going downstairs every night, after she was undressed, to smoke a pipe … The daughter, who lay with her, feel asleep, and did not miss her mother till she awaked in the morning, April 10 1744; when dressing herself, and going downstairs, she found her mother's body lying on the right side, with her head against the grate and extended over the hearth with her legs on the deal floor, and appearing like a block of wood burning with a glowing fire without flame; Upon which quenching it with two bowls of water. The smother and stench thereof almost stifled the neighbours, whom her cries had brought in. The trunk of the body was in manner burnt to ashes, and appeared like a heap of charcoal covered with white ashes. The head, arms, legs and thighs were also very much burnt.

From just the account above, one might conclude that Mrs Pett got too close to the fire and set herself alight. However, we also learn from the article that there had been no fire in the grate and that the only other source of naked flame – a candle – was burnt right down to the bottom of the candlestick. Another interesting observation was that neither the wooden floor, nor a paper screen which was nearby, nor clothing lying next to her had been burnt in any way. It was also said that Mrs Pett had drunk copious quantities of gin the previous evening.

Although the scientists in the mid-eighteenth century concluded only that the fire had been caused by something inside her body, rather than an external catalyst, they could not explain fully the death. At the time, a local rumour was that witchcraft was involved. But from the description of the scene, we can now deduce that poor Mrs Pett died of a phenomenon called spontaneous human combustion.

◦╬◦

On 28 April 2014 a blue plaque was unveiled on what remains of the former Bath Hotel in Felixstowe. It commemorates the centenary of the partial destruction of the hotel by arson. The culprits were two suffragettes and the fire marked the last major action by the women's campaign group before the outbreak of the First World War.

Evaline Hilda Burkitt and Florence Olivia Tunks were accused, tried and convicted at the Bury St Edmunds assizes court in May 1914. They were jailed for two years and nine months respectively for their crime. In the end, neither of them served more than a couple of months of the sentence because they were released under a general amnesty not long after the outbreak of the conflict in August of the same year. The two women had been intent on targeting high-profile tourist venues on the East Anglian coast: earlier in the week they had set fire to Great Yarmouth pier. In Felixstowe they had the choice of three prominent landmarks: the pier, the Spa Pavilion or the fashionable Bath Hotel, which attracted the rich and famous from London.

The Bath Hotel after the fire started by two suffragettes in April 1914.
(Courtesy of Felixstowe Museum Cordy Collection)

The ladies chose the latter, because they knew that it was closed for the season and would therefore be empty of guests. Even though nobody was hurt in the fire, the cost of the damage ran to £35,000.

As with other suffragette actions against high-profile targets, the aim was primarily to make the nation sit up and pay attention to their cause. Burkitt and Tunks were not worried about being caught and even left clues as to the perpetrators of the arson; they hung labels on the bushes in the grounds saying 'votes for women' and there was a banner that said 'there will be no peace until women get the vote'.

It is difficult to tell how the Bath Hotel might have fared had it not become tangled up in the suffragette cause. It had been built in 1839 at a time when planners were establishing Felixstowe as a spa resort. It boasted hot and cold seawater baths. By the end of the nineteenth century though, other grand hotels had been built and were jostling for trade. In the 1920s, the Bartlett Convalescent Home was built on the Bath Hotel site. The hospital closed in 2006 and was converted into luxury apartments.

ૐ

When browsing through the surviving parish registers, which record baptisms, marriages and burials over the centuries, it is not at all unusual to find the baptism of a child and then a burial only a few months (or even days) later. Child mortality was a fact of life. And so the baptism in November 1761 in Wattisham and the subsequent burial in March 1762 of Ann, daughter of John Weatherset, alias Downing, and Mary his wife, appears unremarkable. However, a tragic tale, recorded in gruesome detail at the back of the same register, lies behind these entries.

The narrative begins:

On Sunday January 10 1762, Mary, daughter of John Weatherset alias Downing, aged 16 years, was taken with a pain in her left leg, which in an hour or so sank into her feet and toes. The next day her toes were much swelled and black spots appeared upon them. By degrees the whole feet became swelled and black. The pain which was chiefly in her toes was, she said, as if dogs were gnawing them. The blackness and swelling increased upwards by slow degrees till it came near the knee, and her leg putrefied and came off at the ankle with the foot, leaving the leg bones bare. The other foot and leg were affected in a few days and decayed nearly by the same degrees and manner. Her thighs both swelled under her ham, and an abscess formed.

The surgeon seeing no perfect separation did, on April 17 following, attempt to take off one of the limbs near the knee just above the corrupted flesh, but such an effusion of blood issued as to stop his attempt. He afterwards took off both her legs near the knee. She lived many weeks and then sadly died.

The account continues with similar graphic accounts of similar symptoms endured by both Mary's parents and by her siblings Elizabeth, Sarah, Robert and Edward. The baby Ann's fate is also recorded: 'An infant (Ann) aged two months was taken from the mother's breast as soon as she was seized with the disorder. It was put out to nurse and died within two months. When dead its feet and hands turned black'. All but two of the family died of this mysterious affliction.

In the face of such a tragedy it is heartening that the community reacted with considerable sympathy as the parish clerk reports:

The singularity of the calamity and the smallness of the parish moved many worthy gentlemen to make a collection for the immediate relief and future maintenance of the objects. The sum of about £500 was presently collected out of which a life annuity of 3s per week to each has been purchased for the two surviving girls, that is Elizabeth and Sarah.

A memorial plaque was also erected in the parish church.

Although the villagers at the time had no idea what the cause was, we know now that they had all suffered from ergotism (ergot poisoning) by eating bread made from rye flour ground from seeds diseased by the ergot fungus which develops in a damp grain store. This disease is often known as St Anthony's Fire after an order of monks who specialised in treating ergotism victims across Europe in the Middle Ages and also due to the severe burning sensations in their limbs experienced by sufferers.

❧ FOLLIES ❧

Like many other counties, Suffolk has its fair share of follies. As we know, a folly is essentially a building constructed primarily for decoration, but suggesting through its appearance some other purpose, more often than not grander than the reality. Arguably the most extravagant folly in Suffolk is Freston Tower which overlooks the Orwell estuary. It is a six-storey, red-brick structure with a single, small room on each floor. The twenty-six windows get grander and bigger towards the top.

The six-storey Freston Tower is an impressive sight from the River Orwell.
(Tony Scheuregger)

There is a wonderful, romantic legend attached to Freston Tower, recorded by the Revd Richard Cobbold in his novel *Freston Tower* published in 1850. Cobbold records that the tower was built in the fifteenth century by a Lord de Freston as a place of study and recreation for the lord's only daughter, Ellen de Freston. Every room was dedicated to a different occupation, which claimed its separate hour for work. The lower room was devoted to charity in the reception and relief of the poor; the second to tapestry-working; the third to music; the fourth to painting; the fifth to literature; and the sixth to astronomy, the instruments necessary for which study were fixed upon the turret.

This delightful tale has sadly been disproved by historians, not least because recent tree-ring dating has dated the building to 1578–79, a century later than Cobbold claims it to have been built (although it is possible, of course, that there was an earlier tower on the site). We now know that the present structure was erected by Thomas Gooding, an Ipswich merchant and mercer (a dealer in textiles). With the tower's dramatic positioning overlooking the water, the most compelling theory is that it may have been prompted by Queen Elizabeth I's progress to Ipswich in 1579. This impressive tower, hinting at the wealth and power of the owner, would have been visible from the river upon which the queen may have sailed to enter the town. It would have been quite easy to build it so that it seemed to be attached to a similarly grand mansion!

Over the past few centuries, Freston Tower has been used for a variety of purposes. Today it is owned by the Landmark Trust and is let by them as a holiday home, a far cry from its use in the eighteenth century. In the 1770s the tower and the attached, modest house was used for inoculation of smallpox. The local newspapers of the time carried an advertisement by a Mr Bucke who declares that it is 'now ready for the reception of patients. The best apartments four and five Guineas. Tea, wine and washing excluded. Servants at two Guineas'.

๑๖๑

Two of the most curious follies both appear, on the face of it, to be churches. But they are simply not. The Euston Hall estate has been the family home of the Dukes of Grafton since the 1680s and has, over the centuries, been subject to redesign of the buildings and park by some of the leading architects and landscape gardeners of the age, including William Kent and Capability Brown. Euston's watermill was built in the 1670s to pump water to the park's fountains and to the hall, and to grind corn. But in 1731 it was redesigned by William Kent to resemble a church. That said, the rather plain, red-brick exterior is not a very convincing disguise. Neither does there appear to be a definitive reason for the restyling. And so one must assume that the then Duke of Grafton thought the watermill unsightly.

By contrast, the 'Tattingstone Wonder' has a compelling story to tell. When the White family bought the estate in the 1760s they set about completely rebuilding the manor house, Tattingstone Place, in the new red-brick style. However, Thomas White, like any self-respecting, eighteenth-century squire, wanted a view of the parish church. Since he was clearly unable to move either the church or his new house, he set about building his own 'church'. In around 1790, he took an existing row of three cottages and gave them a facelift. On the crucial north side White erected a fake flint wall, with realistic Gothic windows, and tower. A red, tiled roof completes the 'church'. However, anyone walking around towards the south will find that the tower has only three sides and that the body of the 'church' is nothing more than humble dwellings. The only tell-tale sign evident from the north is a chimney; easily overlooked at a glance. The tradition is that Thomas White commented that since people often wondered at nothing, so he would give them something to wonder about, hence its present-day nickname. Today, the 'church' and the manor house are separated by the Alton reservoir which was created in the 1970s.

∞❦∞

The Suffolk countryside is littered with estate parkland which once surrounded great stately homes, long since demolished by man or destroyed by nature. Of these 'lost' country houses, Rendlesham Hall used to stand in the largest such estate in the county, covering some 250 acres. The hall itself had a rough ride. After a complete rebuild in 1780, the building was destroyed by fire fifty years later only to be reconstructed in a Jacobean style which again burnt down in 1898 and was rebuilt yet again. After the 5th Lord Rendlesham died in 1911 the house was eventually sold for use as a sanatorium until it was requisitioned by the army in the Second World War. When the war was over, no further use was found for the building and it was demolished in 1949.

Thankfully, though, the two estate lodges built in 1790 were left untouched and together form a remarkable pair of follies. Ivy Lodge is a fake ruin with a large archway built to look like it dates from the fourteenth century, and a pseudo-Norman turret. This tower was intentionally built to look like it had suffered the ravages of time. Woodbridge Lodge is a surprisingly different structure. It is a single-storey, hexagonal building with six enormous, stone flying buttresses (such as are normally found supporting great, medieval cathedrals), totally dwarfing the lodge itself. And what are these buttresses supporting? Merely the chimney for the dwelling! This fantastical building simply needs to be seen to be believed.

⚜ GIANTS ⚜

Just outside the porch of the church in Newbourne there are three nineteenth-century gravestones to the Page family. This fact alone is unremarkable until you read the inscription on the one to George Page. Although it is now rather faded, it says: 'Sacred to the Memory of George Page, the Suffolk Giant, Died 20th April 1870, age 26 years. He was exhibited in most towns in England but his best exhibition was with his Blessed Redeemer.' Another clue to his claim to fame is the particularly long gap between this headstone and its accompanying footstone.

George Page and his older brother, Meadows, were both agricultural labourers who were collectively known as 'The Newbourne Giants'. George was 7ft 7in tall when he died, and Meadows was around 7ft 4in. There exists a rather amusing photograph of the two brothers standing either side of their father who stands just above the height of their waists. The two giants were

Page family gravestones in Newbourne churchyard with George Page's headstone and footstone on the left. (Tony Scheuregger)

an attraction at the 1868 Woodbridge Easter Fair when the show's tallest man would hold a guinea above his head and challenge anyone to reach it. They were subsequently hired by Samuel Whiting's Travelling Show and toured with this collection of curiosities for many years. After George's death Meadows continued to tour until 1875 when he settled down to fatherhood back in his home village, where he died in 1917.

As well as being able to visit the brothers' graves in the churchyard, you can also see their childhood house which is next to the village pub, The Fox. Their former home is now appropriately called *The Giant's House*. The inscription on George's tombstone provided inspiration for the author John Owen who lived at nearby Felixstowe. In 1926 he published a novel entitled *The Giant of Oldbourne*.

☙❧

The Port of Felixstowe is the United Kingdom's biggest and busiest container port, dealing with over 40 per cent of Britain's containerised trade. It welcomes over 3,000 ships each year, including the largest container vessels afloat today, due to it having some of the deepest water close to the open sea of any European port. Around thirty shipping lines operate from Felixstowe, offering approximately ninety services to and from some 400 ports around the world. It has its own police, fire and ambulance services. It is undoubtedly one of the most remarkable success stories the county has to tell.

Colonel George Tomline was a Victorian man with a vision. By all accounts he was overbearing and intolerant of any ideas which conflicted with his own. In contrast to this, he was a generous patron. Having bought up every single piece of land he could in and around rural Felixstowe, Tomline set about changing his dreams into reality. He first built a railway line from the sea which linked up with the main line, initially hoping to cash in on the increasing popularity of such seaside resorts for bathing. But because his railway did not go into the centre of the growing town, he decided in 1881 to build a dock at the mouth of the River Orwell. It was a basin 600ft long, 300ft wide with an entrance of 140ft. Protection was provided by two timber piers built on stone and concrete foundations. The dock was opened five years later, in 1886, although Tomline's Fexistowe Dock and Railway Company had been set up under an Act of Parliament in 1875.

Although Colonel Tomline's dock had a bumpy ride during the nineteenth century, it served a useful purpose in the two world wars, but when the site was handed back after war service in 1951, it was very near derelict. Two years later disaster struck in the form of the Great Flood, which almost destroyed the dock. However, its fortunes were reversed very quickly afterwards with a new pier being built in 1956 and through masterful expansion to deal with emerging markets; the labour force ten years later was 230 (as opposed to just nine men in 1955). From here there was no stopping the fastest-growing port in the country and a £3 million project provided a deep water berth and the newest and most expensive container handling equipment. The first Customs House at Felixstowe was opened in 1972. Further development projects, partly funded by the government, have ensured that Felixstowe remains a giant amongst its rivals.

❧

The tiny and stunningly pretty thatched church of Thornham Parva may seem an unlikely place to find one of the most remarkable survivals of sacred medieval art. The priceless framed altarpiece, known as a retable, is the largest and most complete surviving example of its kind. That said, it is still not complete, and historians believe that an altar frontal kept in the Musée de Cluny in Paris goes with it.

But the retable was not always in this small, village church. It is thought that it was painted for a Dominican order of monks at Thetford Priory in Norfolk, and may then have been kept in a private chapel after having been saved from destruction during the Dissolution of the Monasteries by Henry VIII. It shows St Dominic and St Peter Martyr, joint patrons of the Dominicans, and St Catherine and St Margaret of Antioch, who were the order's mascots. The Apostles Peter and Paul are also shown, along with John the Baptist and St Edmund. Experts also believe that the altarpiece may have been painted in the royal workshops as the design is close to that of the sedilia (priests' seats) in Westminster Abbey. The retable was discovered in 1927 in an outbuilding on the Thornham Hall estate. The landowner, Lord Henniker, donated the work of art to Thornham Parva church where his brother was the rector.

In 1994 the retable was moved to the Hamilton Kerr Institute at the University of Cambridge's Fitzwilliam Museum where it underwent seven years of painstaking conservation before being restored to its place behind the altar in the church.

❧

It is well over a century and a half since the mighty Bramfield Oak ceased to be. Alfred Suckling in *The History and Antiquities of the County of Suffolk, Volume 2* describes the moment:

> … on a sultry day, without a breeze to moan its fate, it fell from sheer decay, with a most appalling crash, enveloping its prostrate form with clouds of dust. The exact dimensions of this remarkable tree have not been preserved, but it was asserted at the time of its fall, that a similar bulk of sound timber would have fetched about eighty pounds.

Not only did Bramfield residents boast of the oak's size, but there was also an intriguing legend attached to the tree which suggested that it was over 650 years old when it died. Tradition has it that in 1174 Earl Hugh Bigod fled from the anger of Henry II back to his castle in Bungay. The fifth stanza in an old verse called the Bungay Ballad reads:

When the Baily had ridden to Bramfield oak,
Sir Hugh was at Ilksall bower;
When the Baily had ridden to Halesworth cross,
He was singing in Bungay tower-
'Now that I'm in my castle of Bungay,
Upon the river of Waveney,
I will ne care for the King of Cockney

The mighty Bramfield Oak from Alfred Suckling's *The History and Antiquities of the County of Suffolk, Volume 2.*

Unfortunately recent investigations on the dead trunk, which still stands in the grounds of Bramfield Hall, suggest that the oak was no more than 400 years old, which puts paid to that wonderful story. However, there is a further tale that Elizabeth I once rested underneath its branches. Whilst this, too, is probably only fiction, there is a very small chance that the famous monarch sat under the great Bramfield Oak.

⁂ GRAFFITI ⁂

When we think of graffiti today, the words destructive or unacceptable might come to mind. However, during the Middle Ages it seems that scratching your name, an image or symbol onto the walls and columns in your local parish church was commonplace and almost encouraged. Medieval churches were very different from the plain, whitewashed interiors we see today. Instead, they were a place of vibrancy and colour. Just about every surface would have had some sort of painted decoration on it. Even the lower sections of walls, which would be free from the highly decorative painted schemes, would be colour washed. In light of this, therefore, it is quite surprising to learn that members of church congregations over the centuries carved personal graffiti onto these surfaces. The graffiti inscriptions would therefore have stood out very clearly against the bright pigments of the painted decoration, and they would have been one of the most obvious things people entering the church would have noticed.

This early church graffiti had both meaning and function. Far from being random doodling, they represent the prayers, memorials, hopes and fears of medieval communities. The Suffolk Medieval Graffiti Survey was established in 2014 with the intention of undertaking the very first large-scale survey of early graffiti inscriptions in the county. It is an entirely volunteer-led, community archaeology project that is changing the way we look at our medieval church heritage. To date, over fifty churches have been surveyed and a wide range of graffiti photographed and catalogued.

The walls and pillars inside the church of St Mary, Lidgate, are literally crammed with surviving graffiti. Among these, written in neat, small lettering on a column by the south door, is an intriguing Latin inscription. It translates as 'John Lydgate made this with licence on the day of St Simon and Jude'. Whilst we know which day of the year it was made – 28 October – we do not know the year. We also know a lot about the probable author who was a late-medieval poet, a near contemporary of Geoffrey Chaucer, who lived in the village until he became a monk at the nearby abbey at Bury St Edmunds.

Other graffiti in Lidgate church, mirrored in other Suffolk churches, range from people, fish and other animals, to windmills, ships, mason's and merchant's marks, and crosses and other religious symbols. There is also a magical charm of unknown usage which is almost identical to one found in a manuscript now in the British Library. But by far the cleverest piece of graffiti in Lidgate is one which combines musical notation, an image and text. It is a word puzzle or rebus and has taken some considerable effort to decipher. The first four letters are spelt out: WELL. These are followed, though, by four notes on a musical stave. If these notes are read using the solfège musical teaching system, they spell out FA, RE, MI and LA. The next two letters – DY – are again just spelt out. An image comes next which looks like a gaming die, and can only be

The late medieval rebus inscription in St Mary's church, Lidgate.

understood if you know that the common medieval term for dice was 'cater'. Finally are the letters YNE. So, piecing all these elements together creates the phrase WELL FARE MI LADY CATERYNE (well fare My Lady Catherine). We do not know who scratched this clever piece of graffiti onto a column. Nor do we know when it was done or indeed the identity of Lady Catherine. We can only hazard a guess that it was either a simple message of good wishes or a public declaration of love or devotion. Either way, it gives us a fascinating insight into an unnamed individual who inhabited this small Suffolk village in the Middle Ages.

☙❧

Leaping forward several centuries, in August 2015 a discovery of graffiti at a former Royal Air Force base at Raydon resulted in tracing the 100-year-old widow of an ex-United States serviceman from Oklahoma. 'The Eighth in the East' is a Heritage Lottery-funded project to explore the legacy of the 8th United States Army Air Force's presence in East Anglia during the Second World War. Many hectares of land in the region were used to construct airfields, hospitals, headquarters and bomb stores.

(Courtesy of the Norfolk & Suffolk Medieval Graffiti Survey)

When volunteers were surveying the buildings at Raydon airfield, they found a number of pieces of graffiti. Some were written on brickwork by the bricklayers working to construct the building and by servicemen. Another is scratched into concrete and reads 'BRUCE GLENN, FARGO OKLA, AUG. 24 1943'. From this helpful inscription, the project team were able to discover that Bruce Glenn had been a driver before enlisting in October 1942 and was attached to a fighter squadron that was stationed at RAF Raydon. Although Bruce Glenn died in 2002, the team were able to trace his widow, Clarice. They made contact with Bruce's daughter, Dawn, who was extremely excited about the find and confirmed that it was her father's handwriting.

⁜ HAUNTINGS ⁜

The Ancient House in Ipswich, which has its origins in the fifteenth century, now stands in one of the pedestrianised shopping areas in the centre of town. It is also now a shop. It is not surprising that there are many stories of ghosts associated with the property. But one of these tales may convince some disbelievers in hauntings to read on.

During the mid-seventeenth century, Matthew Hopkins, the self-styled Witchfinder General, struck terror in the hearts of many women in Suffolk. He was responsible for the death of about one hundred accused witches (mostly females), predominantly in East Anglia. In 1645 a woman called Mary Lackland, along with a neighbour, Alice Denham, were accused of

Frontispiece from Matthew Hopkins' *The Discovery of Witches* of 1647.

practising witchcraft. Her accusers believed that she was, amongst other crimes, responsible for the deaths of four people, including her husband. John Lackland had been a barber who with his wife, according to surviving documents, had lived above his business in St Stephens Lane, next to the Ancient House. Mary Lackland was duly found guilty of being a witch and sentenced to death. Although hanging was the usual method of execution for this crime, Lackland was deemed to have committed petty-treason by virtue of her having killed her husband. She was therefore burned at the stake on 9 September 1645.

In 1997, some 350 years after Mary Lackland was put to death, a series of strange, unexplained occurrences took place in the Ancient House. The staff of the shop renting the property found that flowers had been rearranged when no one was in the building, personal belongings disappeared and then reappeared, and a staff member was locked in the cellar until the door inexplicably burst open again. There had long been a tale of a 'Grey Lady' who haunted the house and so the shop manager brought in a spiritualist medium. The medium was able to quickly confirm the presence of a female ghost who was unhappy, and who had died a long time ago. Not much to identify the spirit, then. Apart from, perhaps the name of the retail outlet that occupied the premises which was … Lakeland. Was this a coincidence or, perhaps, a sign of the supernatural at work?

⊙⊙

We are all familiar with stories of haunted buildings. But we are, perhaps, less acquainted with a whole house which is the ghost. But that is exactly what has been happening for over 150 years on a stretch of road between Rougham Green and Bradfield St George.

The story starts in June 1860 when a local farmer called Robert Palfrey was out in the fields one evening. Feeling a sudden and unexplained chill, he looked up to see a large red brick house with gardens in full bloom behind ornate iron gates, where there had been no building at all a moment before. It was to be another fifty-two years, in 1912, before the next sighting, this time by Mr Palfrey's grandson, James Cobbold. Mr Cobbold was riding on a pony trap alongside the village butcher, George Waylett, when they were both startled by a sudden cool breeze and drop in temperature. They also report having heard a whooshing noise. The pony reared in panic and the butcher was thrown to the ground. In that instant, James Cobbold saw a three-storey Georgian mansion, complete with gardens, where there had just been an empty field a moment before. A mist quickly enveloped the house and it was gone before the butcher had had a chance to see it.

The 'Rougham Mirage' (as it is often called) has been sighted a number of times in the past hundred years, For instance, a young teacher, Miss Wynne, was exploring the countryside with one of her pupils in 1926. Some years later she recorded what they had seen:

> We had never previously taken this particular walk, nor did we know anything about the topography of the hamlet of Bradfield St. George. Exactly opposite us on the further side of the road and flanking it, we saw a high wall of greenish-yellow bricks. The road ran past us for a few yards, then curved away from us to the left. We walked along the road, following the brick wall round the bend, where we came upon tall, wrought-iron gates set in the wall. I think the gates were shut, or one side may have been open. The wall continued on from the gates and disappeared round the curve. Behind the wall, and towering above it, was a cluster of tall trees. From the gates a drive led away among these trees to what was evidently a large house. We could just see a corner of the roof above a stucco front, in which I remember noticing some windows of Georgian design. The rest of the house was hidden by the branches of the trees. We stood by the gates for a moment, speculating as to who lived in this large house.

The following spring, Miss Wynne and her charge had taken the same walk and all they saw in the place they had previously seen the house was a wilderness of weeds, mounds of earth and trees.

The most recent sighting was in 2007 when Jean Bartram and her husband were driving along Kingshall Street in Rougham. Mrs Bartram remarked on a beautiful Georgian house with graceful lines, elegant windows and a picturesque garden. However, when the couple returned later that day, the house was nowhere to be seen.

Inevitably there have been investigations undertaken into what these people saw. Although maps dating from after the first sighting confirm that there was and is no such property on the site, an 1815 map suggests that there may have been a large property on or near the field where the mirage was seen. There are also reportedly remains of bricks and tiles in the locality as well as the foundations of a wall. However, clearly even if there was a house there in the early nineteenth century, there were no bricks and mortar there when the mirage was spotted. We await the next sighting with interest.

⚜ HEADS ⚜

Local legend has it that, after being defeated in battle against the Danes, King Edmund of East Anglia (who reigned from AD 855 until his death) hid under the Goldbrook Bridge in Hoxne. The reflection of his golden spurs glinting in the water revealed his hiding place to a newlywed couple crossing the bridge. The couple informed the Danes who promptly captured Edmund and demanded he renounce his faith. When he refused to do so, he was tied to a nearby oak tree. After whipping him, the Danes shot spears at him until he was entirely covered. Even then he would not forsake Christ and so was beheaded and the head was thrown into the woods.

King Edmund's followers had no problem finding his body but his head was missing. Searching for his remains, they heard a cry of 'Here, here, here' and traced the voice to a wolf who was protecting Edmund's severed head. The wolf allowed them to take the head and they buried him nearby, building a wooden chapel over the spot. Many years later, after the threat from the Danes had ceased, they recovered Edmund and found his body was as sound as if he were alive, including a completely healed neck.

Edmund's body was moved several times before finally coming to rest at what is now Bury St Edmunds. Thirty years after his death he was venerated by the Vikings of East Anglia who produced a coinage to commemorate him. As well as the miraculous reinstatement of his body, a number of other miracles are associated with Edmund. St Edmund, as he became after his martyrdom, was the first patron saint of England. Although he has since lost this title to St George, St Edmund remains the patron saint of kings and of pandemics.

A medieval illumination depicting the martyrdom of King Edmund.

In Hoxne a great oak tree stood for around 1,000 years until it fell in 1848. The tree's trunk was over 20ft in circumference. When the tree was cut up, it is said that an old arrowhead was found deep within the tree, 5ft from the base. Today a stone cross marks the spot where the tree stood with an inscription 'St Edmund the Martyr AD 870. Oak tree fell August 1848 by its own weight.' There are, however, several other competing claims to the place of Edmund's death, including Bradfield St Clare. The historians will, no doubt, continue to debate this point.

☙❧

It seems incredulous that the severed skull of a self-declared constitutional head of Great Britain should turn up in the drawing room of a clergyman in Melton. But that is exactly what happened. After the restoration of Charles II as king in 1660, he ordered a posthumous execution at Tyburn in London of Oliver Cromwell, the man who had been responsible for the beheading of his father, Charles I. After hanging, Cromwell was beheaded and his head placed on a 20ft spike above Westminster Hall. Somewhere between 1672 and 1703 (depending on the source) a storm broke the pole and the head ended up in the hands of a succession of private collectors and museum owners until, in 1815, it was sold to Josiah Henry Wilkinson who handed it down as a family heirloom which made its way to Melton in Canon Horace Wilkinson's care.

Determined to obtain a definitive answer as to the authenticity of the head, Canon Wilkinson had it scientifically examined by two eminent surgeons. They noted evidence such as eight axe blows – consistent with the accounts of the beheading – and remains of red hair (as Cromwell had had). They also found evidence of the famous wart on Oliver Cromwell's face. Their 109-page report concluded by saying:

> We started this enquiry in an agnostic frame of mind, tinged only by scepticism as to whether the positive statements made in the past were not based solely on impressions unjustified by any attempt at a scientific investigation. We finish our enquiry with the conclusion that it is a moral certainty drawn from the circumstantial evidence that the Wilkinson head is the genuine head of Oliver Cromwell, Protector of the Commonwealth.

On his death in 1957, Horace Wilkinson bequeathed the head to his son, also called Horace. However, Horace Wilkinson junior wanted to organise a proper burial for the head rather than have it on public display and so he contacted Sidney Sussex College, Cromwell's former college, which arranged a burial. There it was interred on 25 March 1960, in a secret location near the antechapel, preserved in the oak box in which the Wilkinson family had kept the head since 1815. The box was placed into an airtight container and buried with only a few witnesses, including family and representatives of the college. The secret burial was not announced until two years later and the exact whereabouts is not known beyond the few who were present at the ceremony.

⊚⊱⊚

The church of St Gregory in Sudbury is home to the mummified head of a former Archbishop of Canterbury – another rather curious exclusivity Suffolk can lay claim to. Simon of Sudbury, born as Simon Theobald, was born in the town in 1316 and after having entered the Church, progressed through the ranks to the very top. It was Simon of Sudbury who crowned Richard II at Westminster Abbey in 1377.

In 1380, Simon was made Lord Chancellor and therefore became involved with the preoccupations of the financial predicament the government was facing in sustaining its war with France. A controversial poll tax was levied on the population, which resulted in the uprising commonly known as the Peasants Revolt. Many blamed Simon of Sudbury and as a result he was captured and taken to Tower Hill to be beheaded. The execution was messy and clumsy and it took eight strokes of the axe to finally cut off his head. Simon's head was paraded around Westminster and then placed on a pike above the gatehouse on London Bridge, the place where traitors were displayed. A few days later, however, the pole that had held Simon's head displayed the head of Wat Tyler, the overthrown leader of the revolt.

Simon's body was taken to Canterbury where it was buried with great pomp. But instead of a head, they buried him with a cannon ball in its place because Simon's head had been taken and secretly transported to Sudbury where it can still be seen today. Recently a recreation of Simon's head was undertaken by using skeletal detail taken from his part-mummified skull. A forensic artist employed state-of-the-art reconstruction techniques to recreate Sudbury's facial features to complete a series of three-dimensional, bronze-resin casts of his head. These casts were revealed on 15 September 2011 in St Gregory's church, 630 years after Simon's death.

❖ IRON ❖

The name of Garretts in Suffolk is synonymous with the Industrial Revolution. A family whose roots in the county stretch back to the fourteenth century, it seems always to have been a trailblazer in new technology and design. In the eighteenth century, when road travel was becoming vital for industry and communications, Turnpike Trusts were set up by Acts of Parliament to manage stretches of road and to ensure the upkeep of the main highways. From 1767, milestones were compulsory on all such roads, not only to inform travellers of direction and distances, but to help coaches keep to schedule. The distances

A cast-iron milepost made by J. Garrett attached to an earlier stone one in Blythburgh.
(Tony Scheuregger)

were also used to calculate postal charges before the uniform postal rate was introduced in 1840. At their height, there were over 200 milestones in Suffolk, about a half of which survive today. Stone, however, was in short supply in the region and when the lettering on the stones became worn, cast-iron mileposts were made to attach to the existing stone. Many of these were manufactured in Ipswich at the ironworks of Jacob Garrett. These have lasted well and you can spot a number along the present A12, part of which runs along the former Ipswich to Southtown (now Great Yarmouth) Turnpike.

In 1778, Jacob's brother Richard Garrett moved from the family business of tool and machine-making in Woodbridge to nearby Leiston to join forces with a local businessman in his forge in the High Street. Following the death of his business partner in 1782, Richard acquired a larger site and founded what would become Richard Garrett & Sons, 'a general iron works and agricultural implement manufactory'. It was to remain under active Garrett ownership until 1932, when it sadly went into receivership and was bought by Beyer Peacock of Manchester. But in its heyday in the nineteenth and early twentieth century it was one of the best-known manufacturers of steam engines, large numbers of which were exported to all corners of the world. At the Great Exhibition of 1851 in London, Garretts had a prominent and well-stocked stand.

One of Garretts' innovations at the Leiston works was the construction, in the 1850s, of the Long Shop (named after its length). It is one of the earliest examples in the world of a building designed for assembly-line mass production. Although other products, particularly seed drills, continued to be made, the threshing machine and the portable steam engine and then the traction engine and road-building machines were the mainstay of their business.

❧

The coming of the railway – the 'iron road' – undoubtedly had a huge impact on rural Suffolk. Indeed some seaside resorts owed their initial success to the extension of the rail network to the coastal towns. It also transformed the wider landscape by changing agricultural practices. Farming intensified as expanding railway links ensured that farmers could provide freshly picked fruit and vegetables to London, rather than just for local markets.

The Eastern Counties Railway was formed in 1836 with the aim of linking London with Ipswich via Colchester and then onwards to Norwich and Yarmouth. Construction began a year later but was beset by engineering and financial difficulties. And so the railway line did not reach Ipswich until 1846.

In 1862, the Eastern Counties Railway merged with other smaller railways to form the Great Eastern Railway. It was this company which oversaw the rapid expansion of the rail network in Suffolk, reaching all the main towns in the county and passing through many more villages. Eventually declining passenger numbers and financial losses in the late 1950s and early 1960s prompted the closure of numerous branch lines and stations in Suffolk, under the famous 'Beeching Axe'. Some former stations are now private residences, while a number of the lines have been turned into routes for ramblers.

In the early days of the railways, there were the inevitable accidents, some resulting in death such as this one reported on in graphic detail in the *Bury & Norwich Standard* of 22 October 1872:

FATAL ACCIDENT AT IPSWICH STATION – On Wednesday an inquest was held by Mr. Jackaman, Coroner for Ipswich, touching the death of Albert William Chapman, aged 22, one of the porters at the Ipswich passenger station … The Ipswich station is situated within a couple of hundred yards of a tunnel; between the mouth of the tunnel and the platform of the station is a turntable, and it was part of Chapman's duty to assist in turning engines there. He was engaged with three other porters shortly after six o'clock on Tuesday evening in turning two engines, when the whistle of an approaching train in the tunnel was sounded twice, indicating that it was the train which left London at 3.45 p.m. Two of the porters who were at the turn-table ran across the line to the platform, to be ready to attend to their duty on the arrival of the train, and the third called out to Chapman, who stood with one foot over the metals of the down line, 'Look out, the passenger train is coming through the tunnel!' Chapman said to the two men who were running across the line, 'Never mind the train, we must turn the engine.' At that moment, the train emerged from the tunnel, going at about four or five miles an hour. One of the buffers of the engine struck the unfortunate young man on the back and hurled him forward three or four yards. He fell across the metals, and the whole train passed over him, cutting his body completely in two, just above the hips, so that when the train had passed, the trunk lay on one side of the line and the lower part of the body and legs on the other. He, of course, died immediately.

⁂ JAIL ⁂

Nineteenth-century prisons were not designed to offer a pleasant experience for inmates. Nevertheless they were meticulously planned so as to allow good

A prison treadmill, invented by Sir William Cubitt.

management of the various categories of prisoner. One of the largest jails in Suffolk was in Bury St Edmunds and it appears to have been the appointment of John Orridge as governor in 1798 which prompted the decision to construct a new building. The new jail was built during the first years of the nineteenth century to a design by George Byfield and was first occupied by inmates on 8 December 1805. In 1856 a new chapel was built, probably at the north side of the governor's house. The house had an octagonal plan with alternating long and short faces. In each wall there were windows to oversee the yards around the house. There were four detached wings radiating from the house and each was divided longitudinally to allow two categories of inmate to be accommodated. One half of one of the wings was further subdivided to house both female felons and female debtors. Later two smaller blocks to hold female convicts and juvenile offenders were added. The entrance range consisted of a central gate flanked by a turnkey's room and governor's office. Flanking the gate there was a washhouse and brewhouse, with dayrooms beyond these. The prison's facade, one of the only remaining pieces of the building, had a flat platform over the doorway which was used for public executions.

Orridge became a respected authority on prison management, introducing a classification of prisoners. In 1819 he was invited by the government to write a paper on the subject for the Emperor of Russia. In it he describes in minute detail how the governor should run the prison, what the responsibilities of his staff were, and how the prisoners should be treated, housed, clothed and employed. Here is what he says about the treatment of those convicts sentenced to hard labour:

> The several persons who shall be committed to be kept to hard labour, shall be employed (unless prevented by ill-health) every day during their confinement (except Sundays, Christmas Day and Good Friday) for so many hours as the daylight in the different seasons of the year will admit, not exceeding twelve hours, being allowed thereout to rest half an hour at breakfast, an hour at dinner and half an hour at supper.

It was clearly a harsh regime which no doubt became harder with the introduction of the treadmill. This was installed in the mill house in Bury Gaol in 1821, intended for grinding corn and making flour. It was the invention of the engineer Sir William Cubitt who was employed by Ransomes, an iron-founding firm in Ipswich. Cubitt was commissioned by local magistrates to devise a deterrent in an effort to reduce serious crime in Suffolk. What he came up with was a huge revolving cylinder made from iron and wood, with steps like the slats of the paddle wheel. Up to twenty-four men at a time were put to work stepping from one slat to the next. It was described by critics as 'the most tiresome, distressing, exemplary punishment that has ever been contrived by human ingenuity'. Despite this, treadmills were installed in prisons across the country and further afield; a sign that the deterrent effect might have been working albeit at the cost of the suffering felt by the convicts who had to endure this hard labour.

❦

In the nineteenth century, when the prison population was at its peak, some Suffolk jails were clearly in better condition than others. In 1836, George Mann escaped from Woodbridge Gaol by managing to remove one of the iron bars from his cell window. Mann then worked from mid-morning until mid-afternoon to remove 100 bricks from the bottom of his cell wall and then dropped down through the hole into the prison garden. From there he escaped the prison but was found a few hours later and returned to another cell! A report into Mann's escape concluded that no blame could be attached to anyone but it concluded that the walls of the prison were generally unsound; the bricks which the prisoner had removed were soft. The inquiry also found that the wood into which the cell bars were set was rotten. It is therefore surprising that they did not encounter more escapees.

☙❦❧

HM Prison Hollesley Bay, known locally as Hollesley Bay Colony, is an open prison which has had its fair share of media attention. Following an apparently high number of escapes, it acquired its nickname 'Holiday Bay'. Until 2006, it had the largest British prison farm with the oldest established stud for the Suffolk Punch Horse in the world.

One of Hollesley Bay's most high-profile inmates was the Conservative politician and novelist Jeffrey Archer. Archer was convicted of perjury and perverting the course of justice at the Old Bailey in 2001. He spent the last nine months of his sentence at Hollesley Bay before being released in July 2003. Whilst serving his sentence, Archer wrote a three-volume memoir, *A Prison Diary* with volumes named after the first three prisons in which he served time. They were also fashioned after Dante's *Divine Comedy* with the subtitles *Hell, Purgatory* and *Heaven*. None of the three volumes are centered on his short time in the Suffolk prison. However, the last few pages in his final volume describe life there. He had to settle reluctantly for a job as a library orderly, boasting that in his first week in the position only thirty-two books were issued as opposed to 192 books, eight months later. The final chapter of his diary is brief and details his release day:

Day 725, Monday 21 July 2003: 5.09am – I had a good night's sleep and rose early to take a shower. I pack my bags, so that no time will be wasted once the tannoy calls me across to reception. I am touched by how many prisoners come to my room this morning, to shake me by the hand and wish me luck. However, it is not true, as one tabloid suggested, that I was given a guard of honour as I left prison.

❖ JUBILEE ❖

Today when we think about jubilee celebrations, we remember the spectacular pomp and pageantry in 2012 which marked the diamond jubilee of Queen Elizabeth II's accession to the throne. The only other time in British history that a monarch has celebrated a diamond jubilee was in 1897, when Queen Victoria

celebrated hers. The previous
year, Queen Victoria had
surpassed her grandfather,
George III, as the longest-
reigning monarch and she asked
that any special celebrations be
delayed until 1897 to coincide
with her jubilee. There were,
of course, huge local, national
and international celebrations,
parties, commemorative
services and the like. But
many communities across the
country also decided to mark
this moment in history in
bricks and mortar. And Suffolk
has, perhaps, some of the most
stunning of such structures.

Holy Trinity church in Long
Melford is without doubt one
of the finest examples of a
medieval church in the country.
In 1701, however, a lightning
strike damaged the original
tower and it was subsequently
demolished. The new tower
which replaced it, built fifteen
years later, was in red brick, later
covered in cement. By the late
nineteenth century some of the
cement had broken away and
the rather ugly appearance of
the tower was not considered
appropriate for such a grand
church. And so, as part of Queen
Victoria's diamond jubilee
celebrations, Long Melford
villagers set up a committee to

The clock tower in Newmarket erected to
commemorate Queen Victoria's golden
jubilee in 1887. (Tony Scheuregger)

raise funds for a new tower. It took some years to ensure all the funding was in place but the resulting neo-Gothic design matches the old style of the main church. The new tower was dedicated by the bishop in 1903. The pinnacles of the old, brick tower had been removed and new, grander pinnacles were named Victoria, Edward, Alexandra and Martyn in honour of the (then) late queen and the new royal family.

Ten years earlier, in 1887, the nation celebrated Queen Victoria's golden jubilee. Many towns chose to mark the occasion by erecting clocks or clock towers. One of the better known of these remains the most prominent landmark in the town of Newmarket. To commemorate the queen's golden jubilee, Newmarket townspeople established a fund to build the three-tier clock tower in a Gothic style. Although the structure of the tower was paid for by public subscription, a local racehorse trainer donated the clock, which had been made by Smith of Derby. The tower incorporates drinking fountains at the base of three of the faces, and a weathervane with a rider and racehorse on the top. The second stage has a carved inscription which reads '1837 Jubilate Victoriae 1887. Clock presented by C. Blanton. Erected by voluntary contribution'.

ॐ

The silver jubilee of Queen Elizabeth II in 1977 is still remembered by very many Suffolk residents. The monarch visited Ipswich on the afternoon of Monday, 11 July, when a holiday was given to all county council schools. A special, national Jubilee [Bank] Holiday was announced for Tuesday, 7 July. This provided the opportunity for community events to mark the occasion. Unlike Queen Victoria's jubilees, there were no great gestures in the form of monuments and buildings, although the anniversary provided a focus for village signs in the county to be commissioned and unveiled, many coordinated by the local Women's Institute. But in many Suffolk villages and towns, committees were formed and plans drawn up for a real community celebration with the emphasis on having fun.

Leafing through some of the programmes of jubilee events lodged in the Suffolk Record Office, you also get a wonderful sense of Suffolk folk at their very best. Elmswell held a sports day and children's fancy-dress competition followed by a teenage disco in the evening. And the day after, there was an 'Old Fashioned Village Social Evening' organised by the Over 60s Club. Residents also held a quiz and a bowls competition, both of which had a silver cup as the prize. In Clare they held an 'Old Tyme Music Hall' with a reward for the best-dressed lady or gentleman. They also held a pet show, a photographic competition, a tug of war and a 'Comic Football Match'. But a special mention must be given to Long Melford who, alongside Punch & Judy shows and a pram race, hosted Welly Wanging and Tossing the Sheaf!

⁘ KEYS ⁘

The tiny Shelland church is unusual in a number of respects. To start with, it is dedicated to King Charles the Martyr. Although King Charles I, who was executed in 1649, was never officially canonised by the Church of England, six churches across the country are dedicated to him. Secondly, until 1936 it was a donative living: a church building erected by a private landowner who appointed his own choice of minister. And thirdly, it has one of the last barrel organs in regular use in the country. At first glance it may appear similar to any other village church organ. But on closer inspection it is evident that there is no keyboard!

The barrel organ behind the font in Shelland church. (Tony Scheuregger)

The barrel organ was made by the firm of H. Bryceson in 1810, at a time when local instrumentalists in churches were being replaced by organs. It stands 7ft high and has three original wooden barrels, studded with spikes varying in size. Each barrel contains twelve tunes, thus allowing for thirty-six tunes in total. The 'organist' operates a handle which turns the barrel and fills the bellows with air. The air is then passed from the bellows to the thirty-one pipes. Although the organ grinder does not have any control over the tune, he has six stops which govern the volume and tone.

⚜

Not many parish churches in the country can boast a treasure so rare that it is housed in the British Museum. However, one which can is Eyke. The village name derives from the word 'oak' and various different spellings have been used over the centuries including Eike, Yke, Ike and Eych. At a time when each parish church was at the centre of community life, many important documents relating to the business undertaken were housed in the parish chest. Although these chests were locked, the churches themselves, many with items of great value, also had to be secured. When the parish officers at Eyke commissioned a new key for the church door in the fifteenth century, they arranged for its wards (the unique configuration of its locking mechanism) to spell the word 'Ike' when viewed from the side. The door lock has since been changed but a replica of the original key hangs inside the church.

◈

It is an undisputed fact that it was a dentist's son from Lowestoft who made Suffolk the heart of the twentieth-century British musical landscape. His name was Benjamin Britten; the composer, conductor and pianist who was the first composer to be given a life peerage. Aside from his musical compositions – including opera, vocal music, orchestral and chamber pieces – he is best remembered for his founding of the annual Aldeburgh Festival in 1948 and the creation of Snape Maltings concert hall. At the festival, Britten and his companion, the tenor Peter Pears, brought together international stars and emerging talent from around the world.

By the 1960s, the Aldeburgh Festival was outgrowing its usual venues in the region and original plans to build a new concert hall in Aldeburgh were not progressing. And so when redundant Victorian maltings buildings in the village of Snape, 6 miles inland, became available for hire, Britten realised that the largest of them could be converted into a concert hall and opera house. The 832-seat Snape Maltings Hall was opened by Queen Elizabeth II at the start of the twentieth Aldeburgh Festival on 2 June 1967 and was immediately hailed as one of the best concert halls in the country. The hall was destroyed by fire in 1969, but Britten was determined that it would be rebuilt in time for the following year's festival, which it was. The queen again attended the opening performance in 1970. The maltings gave the festival a venue that could comfortably house large orchestral works and operas, and it continues to host world-class performers under its current management, Aldeburgh Music.

Snape Maltings concert hall. (Tony Scheuregger)

In September 2015 an old red phone box situated at Snape Maltings (which had been used since 1990 to provide a hotline to the box office, 5 miles away) was turned into a 'virtual reality concert hall' by installing a headset which allows visitors to listen to and view 360-degree footage of an orchestral performance recorded in the maltings. The user can move the camera to offer different views of the stage and audience.

❧ KINGS ❧

With a reign of just 325 days, Edward VIII was one of the shortest-reigning monarchs in British history. Although he was never crowned in a traditional coronation ceremony, he assumed the throne on 20 January 1936 on the death of his father, Edward VII. A set of four postage stamps were issued with his profile portrait on. In addition, some 271 letterboxes bearing his regnal number were manufactured. Most of these were pillar boxes, whilst six were wall boxes and 104 were so-called 'Ludlow' boxes which were used at sub-post offices. Many of these letterboxes have since disappeared, many being replaced by more modern types. And it is believed that there are only two surviving examples of the 'Ludlow' type, one of which is at Bawdsey, on the Suffolk coast near Felixstowe. Sadly, the metal plate was stolen some years ago but has been replaced by a replica bearing the same royal cipher ('EVIIIR') and writing.

Curiously, it was in Felixstowe that Edward VIII's future wife, Wallis Simpson, chose to live for six weeks in the autumn of 1936 in order to gain the necessary residential qualifications to have her divorce hearing held in Ipswich. Mrs Simpson stayed at Beach House in Undercliff Road East and although the house is no longer there (it was demolished after an arson attack in 1989), in 2012 a plaque was put up on the spot where the house stood commemorating this famous short-term resident. As one might imagine, Wallis Simpson did not like out-of-season 1930s Felixstowe, cut off from the national and international social scene in a five-bedroom house. She wrote in her autobiography:

The rare 'Ludlow'-type letterbox in Bawdsey bearing the cipher of Edward VIII. (Tony Scheuregger)

My first glimpse of the little house in Felixstowe was dismaying. It was tiny; there was barely room for the three of us [two friends and herself], plus a cook and a maid, to squeeze into it. There is nothing drearier than a resort town after the season. The only sounds were the melancholy boom of the sea breaking on the deserted beach and the rustling of the wind around the shuttered cottages. When I walked down to town for the mail and the newspapers not a head turned at our passage. On fair days, we used to walk alone on the beach and for all the attention ever paid to us, we could have been in Tasmania.

Edward VIII used to visit her in Felixstowe; his plane would land on the nearby cliffs and he would go to the local hotel to have a few pints with the locals.

The divorce court in the county town of Suffolk was chosen as it was hoped that it would be a low-key affair. Unfortunately, though, the world's press had been alerted and Ipswich was besieged. The hearing itself lasted only twenty-five minutes after which Wallis Simpson fled to the more comfortable and familiar capital.

In the past, the main way in which gentry wishing to impress the monarch could do so was by offering lavish and expensive (for the host!) entertainment when the king or queen was passing through the county. Some were more successful than others, and none it seems more so than the Crofts family of Little Saxham Hall. There, in a country estate now long since disappeared, generation after generation of this family opened up their residence to royalty. It was ideally situated so as to allow easy access to Newmarket where the Stuart kings spent much of their leisure time.

Charles II stayed at Saxham Hall on at least four occasions and it appears that a good time was had by all. During one of the visits Lord Arlington, a member of the King's Privy Council who travelled with the monarch, wrote, 'I could not speak to the king at Saxham, nor until today, by reason of the uncertainty of his motions'. And the famous diarist Samuel Pepys also accompanied the king there in 1668, recording after the event:

> That the King was drunk at Saxam … the night that my Lord Arlington come thither, and would not give him audience, or could not which is true, for it was the night that I was there, and saw the King go up to his chamber, and was told that the King had been drinking. He tells me, too, that the Duke of York did the next day chide Bab. May for his occasioning the King's giving himself up to these gentlemen, to the neglecting of my Lord Arlington: to which he answered merrily, that, by God, there was no man in England that had heads to lose, durst do what they do, every day, with the King, and asked the Duke of York's pardon: which is a sign of a mad world. God bless us out of it!

Indeed in Pepys' original diary manuscript, there are several blank pages with no entries between 29 September and 11 October 1668, some think because there was so much drunkenness and debauchery during the visit that Pepys could not bring himself to record it. It is more likely, though, that the diarist had been visiting family in the neighbourhood.

Pepys was also present in April 1670 when he records that King Charles was entertained at Lord Crofts' on the Saturday evening and attended church at Little Saxham church the next day. Whether it was the tedium of the lengthy sermon or the effects of the excess alcohol from the previous night (or perhaps both!), it is rumoured that the king nodded off, subsequently having to ask for the priest's homily to be printed.

❧

The Borough of St Edmundsbury, the authority which runs the cathedral town of Bury St Edmunds, has as its motto *Sacrarium Regis, Cunabula Legis* which means 'Shrine of a King, Cradle of the Law'. Whilst the first part of the phrase refers to the martyred King Edmund whose shrine was housed in the town's abbey, the second lays claim to its crucial role in the drawing up of the Magna Carta.

By the autumn of 1214, there was widespread discontent in England. King John's subjects simply felt that they had suffered enough under his harsh rule and the heavy financial obligations they faced. And so in November 1214, John's opponents met in the abbey at Bury St Edmunds. The chronicler Roger of Wendover in his *Floes Historiarum* (The Flowers of History) takes up the story:

> About this time the earls and barons of England assembled at St Edmund's as if for religious duties, although it was for some other reason; for after they had discoursed together secretly for a time, there was placed before them the charter of King Henry the First, which they had received, as mentioned before, in the City of London from Stephen, Archbishop of Canterbury. This charter contained certain liberties and laws granted to the holy church as well as the nobles of the kingdom, besides some liberties which the king added of his own accord. All therefore assembled in the church of St. Edmund the king and martyr, and commencing from those of the highest rank, they all swore on the great altar that, if the king refused to grant these liberties and laws, they themselves would withdraw from their allegiance to him, and make war on him, till he should, by a charter under his own seal, confirm to them everything they required; and finally it was unanimously agreed that, after Christmas, they should all go together to the king and demand the confirmation of the aforesaid liberties to them, and that they should in the meantime provide themselves with horses and arms so that if the king should endeavour to depart from his oath, they might by taking his castles compel him to satisfy their demands; and having arranged this, each man returned home.

The exact date of this meeting of the barons is not known, although historians believe the most likely date was 20 November 1214, the Feast of St Edmund and therefore the most likely cause for a congregation of the great and the good of the land. A plaque on one of the surviving abbey nave columns marks this event. The following year, and as a direct result of this meeting in Bury St Edmunds, King John sealed the Magna Carta. It confirms Suffolk's key role in the bitter struggle for power and justice which, in the following 800 years, influenced ideas of liberty, human rights and even political systems across the world.

❖ LINES ❖

A rather surprisingly talented shoemaker and seller of boot blacking called Samuel Hart lived in the village of Kettleburgh in the mid-nineteenth century. Whilst census returns offer no clues as to his gifts beyond making and repairing footwear, it appears that he had various sidelines. In White's *Directory of Suffolk* of 1844, he is described as an herbalist and poet. He apparently advertised himself as a 'Curer of bunions, scab heads, rheumatism, scrofula and various other complaints incidental to the human frame. Poems and Pieces composed and arranged for any occasion'. And it seems that Samuel Hart did indeed cater for all eventualities: if his cures did not work, then he would compose an epitaph for the gravestone! His literary genius lives on chiselled into the local gravestones, including one for William Turner, son of Samuel and Maria Turner, who died in 1833 aged 18:

> Short was my life yet long my rest may be
> Cut off in youth, as you may plainly see
> Nursed up with care, and parents dear had I,
> They loved me well and grieved to see me die.

There is also this one for Hannah, wife of William Farthing, who died in 1854:

> Her last words when on her deathbed lie,
> She spoke plain and not bewilderin:
> She said dear husband I must die;
> Pray provide for my poor children.

❦

George Crabbe was an Aldeburgh-born poet, surgeon and clergyman whose work *The Borough* is immortalised in Benjamin Britten's opera *Peter Grimes*. *The Borough* is a collection of poems published in 1810 arranged in a series of twenty-four letters. They cover various aspects of borough life, clearly using Aldeburgh as his inspiration. Some of the letters are stories on inhabitants' lives, Peter Grimes being one of them, another being about Abel Keene, a village schoolmaster and then a merchant's clerk who is led astray, loses his employment and hangs himself.

Crabbe's *The Village* is an equally enthralling glimpse of rural life in the late eighteenth century. In this extract, he paints a vivid picture of the village poorhouse:

The poet George Crabbe (1754–1832).

Theirs is yon House that holds the parish poor,
Whose walls of mud scarce bear the broken door;
There, where the putrid vapours, flagging, play,
And the dull wheel hums doleful through the day;-
There children dwell who know no parents' care;
Parents, who know no children's love, dwell there!
Heart-broken matrons on their joyless bed,
Forsaken wives, and mothers never wed;
Dejected widows with unheeded tears,
And crippled age with more than childhood fears;
The lame, the blind, and, far the happiest they!
The moping idiot, and the madman gay.

The Michael Ley Line will not be unknown to some readers. It runs in a straight line from St Michael's Mount in Cornwall to Hopton-on-Sea on the Norfolk coast (although the civil parish was, until 1974, in the county of East Suffolk). It derives its name from the fact that its line follows the path of the sun on 8 May which is the spring festival of St Michael. And there are many sites devoted to St Michael (and St George) on its 350-mile course. There have been many theories propounded in the past, many with mystical connotations, as to the significance of the line. It was thought to simply be a part of an ancient system of straight trackways used by traders.

The ley line intersects a great many mounds and sacred sites including the abbey ruins in Bury St Edmunds. Here is a mound topped with oak trees. Although it is not a natural feature, it is clear that the monks who constructed the abbey deliberately built around it, hinting at sacred significance. After intersecting Botesdale, Thornham Magna, Eye (through the castle, church and priory ruins) and Hoxne, it passes through the grounds of the twelfth-century St George's church in St Cross South Elmham. Here is a possible ancient stone which may have been one of a large number of such marker stones along the ley line route. Such stones were generally selected for their shape so that they did not have to be worked by a mason. Depending on the part of the country they are found in, marker stones may be pudding shaped, altar shaped or flat topped. We know that many of these stones were transported from some distance away, being of different rock type than the local stone. The South Elmham one comprises a small flat stone set upon a larger one to make a mushroom shape.

☙❦❧

Robert Bloomfield was the so-called 'ploughman poet' who wrote the highly successful 'The Farmer's Boy' in 1800. He was born in 1761 in Honington into a labouring-class family. His father died of smallpox when Robert was young and so his mother supported the six children by teaching at the village school and by spinning. And so he received a basic education from his mother despite being apprenticed at the age of 11 to work on a nearby farm. It was these early experiences of life in rural Suffolk that were to stay with Bloomfield throughout his career. Proving too frail for farm work, he was sent to London to learn to be a shoemaker. One of his duties was to read the papers aloud while the others in the workshop were working, and he became particularly interested in the poetry section of *The London Magazine*.

Bloomfield's poem 'The Farmer's Boy', describing in verse the countryside in four seasons, was a remarkable success, with over 25,000 copies being sold in the first two years. Within three years it had run to seven editions and had been translated into German, French, Italian and even Latin. The celebrated Suffolk-born painter, John Constable, greatly admired the poem and used couplets from it as tags to two of his paintings. It paints a rather idyllic picture of rural life which, nevertheless, provides the reader with a vivid picture of the various scenes he writes about. In this one, Giles (the farmer's boy) chops up turnips to feed to the livestock during the winter months:

On GILES, and such as Giles, the labour falls,
To strew the frequent load where hunger calls.
On driving gales sharp hail indignant flies,
And sleet, more irksome still, assails his eyes;
Snow clogs his feet; or if no snow is seen,
The field with all its juicy store to screen,
Deep goes the frost, till every root is found
A rolling mass of ice upon the ground.
No tender ewe can break her nightly fast,
Nor heifer strong begin the cold repast,
Till Giles with pond'rous beetle foremost go,
And scatt'ring splinters fly at every blow;
When pressing round him, eager for the prize,
From their mixt breath warm exhalations rise.

⁂ LOST ⁂

The Suffolk coastline has not only been threatened by erosion for centuries, the shape of the county's shore has been altered by the ravages of both the sea and the weather. Easton Bavents was once the most easterly parish in England. In the sixteenth century, it had a thriving harbour, weekly market, church and chapel. Today, the former village is under the North Sea over a mile from the current coastline. Similarly, at Aldeburgh the surviving sixteenth-century Moot Hall (now a museum), which stands alongside the beach, was once in the town centre. And Sizewell, now host to two nuclear power stations, was once a busy fishing village.

Without doubt the most famous of these 'lost' villages of Suffolk is Dunwich. It has a dramatic story to tell. At the time of Domesday Book in 1086 it was a thriving town with three churches. However, even then there was evidence of significant coastal erosion: 'The land on the cliff used to be 200 acres, as the Sea had carried off the other 100.' At the same time as the cliffs were being worn away, though, a spit of land was being created which would provide a perfect harbour. In the next few centuries, Dunwich became a highly successful fishing and mercantile trading port. By 1250 it was one of the largest ports in England with a population of 4,000 people in thirteen parishes.

Dunwich's decline began in 1286 when a storm hit the Suffolk coast. This was followed by two further storms a year later. As a result of this extreme weather, the Dunwich river's exit into the sea shifted a few miles north to Walberswick. Coupled with the destruction of the safe harbour and buildings in Dunwich, the maritime business in the town started to take a rapid downturn. Most of the medieval buildings have disappeared into the sea, including all eight churches. Today, Dunwich has barely a hundred people on its electoral roll, and fewer than fifty permanent residents. Since Roman times, the sea has claimed more than 2km of coastline and reduced a great port to a tiny fishing village.

☙❧

The Suffolk landscape has, as you might imagine, altered greatly over time. And the great manorial houses and estates in the county have been subject to constant reshaping and rebuilding. Over the centuries, these country houses had provided a focus for the communities they governed, providing employment for many. There are still some extremely fine examples of Suffolk country houses: Ickworth House, Melford Hall, Heveningham Hall, Somerleyton Hall and Euston Hall to name but a few. But many more have disappeared from view entirely, lost to the twenty-first century. The tragedy is that some forty of these vanished during the twentieth century, some through fire, although far more through demolition.

The story of Redgrave Hall is typical of the history and fate of one of these country houses. The Redgrave Park estate, which comprises some 200 acres of land and 50 acres of water, is thought to have been first built on in the thirteenth century. The Abbot of Bury St Edmunds, to whom the manor belonged, constructed a stone and timber lodge where he could overnight whilst hunting the deer in the park. At the Dissolution of the Monasteries by Henry VIII, the king granted the estate to Sir Nicholas Bacon (who was to become Lord Keeper of the Privy Seal under Elizabeth I). Bacon rebuilt the house in characteristic Tudor style. The stone he used came from a former hospital in Bury

St Edmunds he had bought and other loads of stone were brought from dissolved local priories and nunneries. The bricks were manufactured on the estate and the timber came from nearby woods at Redgrave, Hinderclay and Rickinghall. The small red tiles used to roof the house came from a kiln at Wyken. Many items were manufactured on or near the site: the lead gutters and conduits, the laths and some of the ironwork. Local craftsmen were used for the jobs where they had the skill to do so, while experts were brought from further afield. The resulting structure was a symmetrical 'C' shape with a clock tower in the centre.

Redgrave Park remained in the Bacon family through 1702 when mounting mortgages forced Sir Robert Bacon, the 5th baronet, to sell. It was bought by Sir John Holt, the Lord Chief Justice. It was Sir John's great nephew, Rowland Holt, who commissioned the famous landscape gardener Lancelot 'Capability' Brown to remodel the hall and park in the fashionable classical Palladian style at a cost of £30,000. The hall was rebuilt in white Woolpit brick. The new house had four ionic pilasters supporting a triangular pedimented facade displaying the Holt family coat of arms and was centered on a central courtyard. The result was a compact and imposing focal point set in the beauty of ancient parkland. Brown remodelled the park, keeping the ancient trees, but adding extra clumps and shelterbelts. He planted other trees in scenic places, and he dammed the stream running through the park to produce the sinuous, 50-acre lake, which included two islands. Brown also built a Palladian 'rotunda' or roundhouse in

Redgrave Hall in the early 1800s. (Courtesy of the Holt-Wilson family archive)

one corner of the park, and a 'water house' (later known as the kennels) and a boathouse beside the lake. A large orangery and a red brick stable block were also built nearer to the hall.

The Redgrave estate remained in the ownership of the Holt-Wilson family until 1971. Beset by financial difficulties, through the second half of the nineteenth century and the first half of the twentieth century, the family eventually sold the now-dilapidated hall for demolition in the 1940s. Originally, the surviving part of Sir Nicholas Bacon's Tudor house was saved in the hope of refurbishing it to provide more modest accommodation. But this sadly never happened and the remains of the house were demolished in 1970. Today only Capability Brown's roundhouse and the 'kennel' survive: a sad but familiar story of a once great estate with significant historical and architectural interest.

❖ MISERS ❖

The county of Suffolk is not particularly well known for its parsimony. However, two of the most famous misers in England took their last breath in Suffolk. William Jennens of Acton Hall near Long Melford was reportedly in his 100th year when he died in 1798. The *Bury and Norwich Post* advising of his death gave an inkling of the trouble ahead:

> He was reputed to be the richest commoner in England, his property exceeding two million pounds sterling. And there is reason to apprehend he died intestate, though it is thought an unexpected will was found amongst his papers in which he devised some comparatively inconsiderable legacies to gentlemen in the neighbourhood … During the long period of his existence he remained a bachelor and more given to penuriousness than hospitality, of course his accumulations magnified even beyond his power of computation. He is reported to have kept 50,000 pounds in bankers' hands for sudden emergencies and never drew out the dividends of his funded property till half a year after they were due.

Jennens was a well-connected man. One of his godfathers had been King William III and he had served as page to George I. Among valuables discovered in his house was a silver pitcher given to Jennens as a christening gift by King William. William Jennens had never married and, on inheriting Acton Hall from his father, Robert, in 1725 abandoned his father's refurbishment plans. Instead, he lived in unfurnished rooms in the basement with his servants and dogs, shunning visitors and social contact. Despite this rather eccentric behaviour he was appointed High Sheriff of Suffolk in 1754. As well as squirrelling away inheritances, Jennens had lent money to gamblers in the London casinos.

And so with William Jennens' death started a long, protracted legal wrangle in the Court of Chancery between various parties who believed they were the heirs to his fortune. Initially Lord Curzon, a descendent of Jennens' aunt, was declared the heir. But this was disputed by numerous nephews and nieces. In July 1805, it was announced in a local newspaper that three soldiers from the East Suffolk Militia had come into large fortunes 'proved to be legal by the representatives of the late William Jennens' but for whatever reason their claim was clearly disproved as the court case rumbled on for many years after this. As late as 1875, a female descendent of one of William's brothers, who lived in America, petitioned the English courts in a bid to claim the money. All this time, although Jennen's fortune had been accruing interest, it was not enough to keep pace with the lawyers' bills and in 1915 the case was finally abandoned when the funds simply ran out.

It is believed that this famous case provided the inspiration for Charles Dickens' ninth novel, *Bleak House*, which was first published in monthly instalments in 1852–53. The central plot involved a long-running legal dispute over inheritance: Jarndyce vs Jarndyce.

The moral of this sad tale is to ensure you make a will, and it appears that William Jennens so nearly did so. *The Gentleman's Magazine*, in recording the miser's demise in 1798, reported: 'A will was found in his coat-pocket, sealed, but not signed; which was owing, as his favourite servant says, to his master leaving his spectacles at home when he went to his solicitor for the purpose of duly executing it, and which he afterwards forgot to do.'

ണ്ട്

Believe it or not, Jennens was not the only eighteenth-century Suffolk miser to have influenced Charles Dickens' writings. John Elwes MP is supposed to have been the inspiration for the character of Ebenezer Scrooge in *A Christmas Carol*. And some years later, Dickens made reference to Elwes in his last novel, *Our Mutual Friend*.

John Elwes was born John Meggot and, by all accounts, inherited his miserliness from his immediate family. His maternal grandmother, Lady Isabella Hervey, was a notorious penny pincher and his mother reputedly starved herself to death because she was too mean to buy food. Elwes came into his first fortune at the age of 4 when his father died in 1718. And then his mother left him another tidy sum. The greatest influence on John's life was his parsimonious uncle, Sir Harvey Elwes of Stoke College in Stoke-by-Clare, who was also MP for Sudbury. John changed his surname to Elwes in order to inherit his uncle's estate worth more than £250,000. He also stepped into his uncle's miserly shoes, living a frugal existence at Stoke College.

John Elwes MP (1714–1789) who was said to have been the inspiration for Dickens' Ebenezer Scrooge.

Elwes was a man of contradictions. At home he went to bed when darkness fell so as to save on candles, and he ate very little apart from mouldy meat and stale bread. However, when out on the town with friends he feasted with them. He wore ragged clothes whilst on his own but dressed in the height of fashion when visiting London friends. Elwes was not a loner, though, and loved to hunt and shoot. And he was far from mean to his associates, lending them huge sums of money, much of which was never repaid. Yet John let his spacious country house become uninhabitable rather than spend the money on necessary repairs. He lived on just £50 per week.

When the unmarried John Elwes died in 1789 he left around £500,000 to his two illegitimate sons, who he reportedly loved but would not educate, believing that 'putting things into people's heads is the sure way to take money out of their pockets'. After his death, his friend Edward Topham (who even published an account of his acquaintance's life) said: 'He lent much to others; to himself he denied everything. But I have not in my remembrance one unkind thing that ever was done by him.'

❖ MONSTERS ❖

Monsters are usually confined to the pages of novels. And so it was not surprising that in July 1912, Lilias, the 19-year-old daughter of adventure writer H. Rider Haggard, found it hard to get the public to take her seriously when she claimed to have seen a sea serpent off the Suffolk cost at Kessingland. However, at least it provided fodder for 'silly season' journalism across the country. Reproduced below is the full report from the *Sheffield Evening Telegraph*:

THE SPEEDY SERPENT: Provides Silly Season Topic at the Seaside.

'Have you seen the sea serpent?' The question is popular at the seaside now since, as we announced in our editions yesterday, the shy old sinner has been sighted for the first time this season. He was first seen by Miss Rider Haggard.

But she is not alone. It seems that a similar experience befell Mr C.G. Harding, of the Lowestoft Water and Gas Company, who on Sunday saw what resembled 'a black line darting along the surface of the water' at a terrific rate. 'It simply went whizzing past,' said Mr Harding, 'as if it were a torpedo which had been discharged along the surface of the water.' Mr Harding quite agreed with the description given by Miss Rider Haggard.

Mr F. Muller, of 28 West Ella Road, Craven Park, writes to *The Daily Chronicle*: - I recently returned from a holiday at Southwold (which is a few miles south of Kessingland), and whilst there saw on two occasions the 'apparition' which Miss Rider Haggard describes. The first time was from the beach, the second from the deck of a steamer between Lowestoft and Southwold. I was in some doubt as to what it could be, for the speed was very great, and unfortunately I had no glasses, but before it left the field of vision the line twisted and rose a little way from the water. My own impression is that the 'sea serpent' was a row of birds flying very swiftly just over the surface of the water. Had it been a 'serpent' there would surely have been some wash visible even from the distance I was situated, and the same applies, I should say, to a school of porpoises.

There are other sceptics besides Mr Muller. Here is what one correspondent says he saw: – 'The mystery cleared, however, on using the glasses which fortunately we had with us. The object was a line, or V-shaped flock, of birds, flying very low and in very much the same rapid and even manner as wild duck. What birds they were I am quite unable to say. But of the fact that they were birds I have no doubt whatever.'

This is bad enough. But there are actually people who decline to believe even in the existence of the sea serpent. Among these is an expert at the Natural History Museum. The 'faithful' are indignant at this attitude. They are now calling on the serpent to put on his full speed – sixty miles an hour – and appear at once and so confound the cynics.

Lilias M. Rider Haggard went on to become a novelist herself (as well as her father's biographer). I wonder whether she ever had second thoughts about her sighting, thinking back perhaps to the bedtime stories her father must have told her when she was younger.

❧

There is a remarkable entry in the parish register of Kelsale which is a translation from an earlier entry written in Latin in the same book. It reads:

> In June was born a wonder, a monster, whose father was Richard Baldwey of Kelsale, begotten in lawfull matrimonie, which childe from the sholders upwards had growinge ij [2] severall necks with ij [2] fayre heds standing upon them in licke quantity eche heade having moths, nose, eies, eares, and winde pipes goying downe in ye throte into ye breste, whose body was licke the forme & shape of all other children which was sene by many credable people of Kellsall.

This event occurred in 1545 and tells a sad tale of how the unexplained was viewed in past centuries. Today, conjoined twins are still unusual but are hardly viewed as freaks of nature as they were in the time of Henry VIII. In fact, other similar entries in different Suffolk parish registers testify to the fact that for at least the next two centuries, conjoined twins were treated with extreme caution and suspicion. In Long Melford, the following burial is recorded: '1618 April 26 Rose, the wife of William Sheap, was delivered of a childe with 2 faces, 4 armes and 4 legges'. It is not at all clear from this entry whether both mother and child died and were buried together: there is no explanatory detail. And in October 1661, the incumbent of St Mary's Woodbridge baptised 'a monstrous child having foure arms, 4 shoulders, 4 thighs & feet but one next & head' which was recorded as stillborn.

Whilst a number of accounts describe such offspring as 'monsters', a record by one rector, made some time after the event, recounts how:

> On Tuesday 26 July 1759 was born in the Parish of Hawstead a Child (or rather two children joined together) with two heads, four arms, four legs. The two faces, which were quite distinct and beautiful were opposite each other. The bodies were united from a little below the necks to somewhat lower than the navels. Both the children of which this monster was formed were males. It was doubtful whether it was born alive, however the mother was certain that it was alive the day before its birth.

Woodcut of conjoined brothers from the *Nuremberg Chronicle* of 1493.

It is refreshing therefore to find a more enlightened view on the birth of conjoined twins, as well as some fascinating anatomical details.

On a more distasteful note, however, a certain Dr Studd of Saxmundham paid for advertising space in the *Norwich Mercury* newspaper in 1736, claiming that he had in his possession 'one of the greatest Curiosities in Nature, being a Double Foetus of a BOY and a GIRL, joined together'. He had apparently delivered the babies some months earlier and had preserved them so that they could be viewed by the paying public.

৹৳৹

Ever since the written word has been used to record events, chroniclers have clearly kept an eye out for the curious and spectacular as well as the more mundane occurrences such as battles, power struggles and royal succession. Two such chronicles point to an interesting dragon 'hotspot' on the border of Suffolk and Essex near Sudbury.

The first account involved Sir Richard Waldegrave, a Member of Parliament for Suffolk and Speaker of the House of Commons, in 1405. Sir Richard lived at Smallbridge Manor near Bures and encountered the monster first-hand. The chronicle reveals:

> Close to the town of Bures there has lately appeared … a dragon vast in body with crested head, teeth like a saw and tail extending to an enormous length. Having slaughtered the shepherd it devoured very many sheep. There came forth an order, to shoot at him with arrows, to the workmen on whose domain he had concealed himself being Sir Richard de Waldegrave, Knight, but the dragon's body although struck by the archers remained unhurt, for those arrows bounced off his back if it were been iron or hard rock. Those arrows that fell upon the spine gave out as they struck it a ringing or tinkling sound just as if they had hit a brazon plate and then flew away off by reason of the hide of the great beast being impenetrable. There was an order to destroy him in all the country people assembled. But when the dragon saw he was again to be assaulted he fled away into a marsh or mere and was no more seen.

And some forty-four years later, according to an account in a manuscript now in the library of Canterbury Cathedral, a battle of the fire-breathing monsters occurred:

On Friday the 26th of September in the year of our Lord 1449, about the hour of
Vespers, two terrible dragons were seen fighting for about the space of one hour,
on two hills, of which one, in Suffolk, is called Kydyndon Hyl and the other in
Essex Blacdon Hyl. One was black in colour and the other reddish and spotted.
After a long conflict the reddish one obtained the victory over the black, which
done, both returned into the hills above named whence they had come, that is to
say, each to his own place to the admiration of many beholding them.

From such seemingly accurate eyewitness records, how can we possibly not
believe in these wonderful mythical creatures?

❖ NAPOLEON ❖

With an open coastline of approximately 49 miles looking out to the European
mainland, Suffolk has always been vulnerable to attack. It has therefore been
subject to fortifications since the late 1400s. But none of the various defence
schemes which were designed are more striking than the surviving Martello
towers. The threat of invasion by Napoleon in the late eighteenth and early
nineteenth centuries led to one of the biggest programmes of coastal defence

The quatrefoil-shaped Martello tower at Slaughden. (Tony Scheuregger)

building in the country up to this point. A string of Martello towers started to be built which stretched eastward along and up the coast form Sleaford in Sussex.

The *Ipswich Journal* of 18 June 1808 reported that Essex and Suffolk were to be fortified to add to the seventy-three towers already built along the south coast. The idea for the towers came from a defensive structure at Mortella in Corsica which the British Navy had found to their cost was able to withstand heavy bombardment. Each structure had 24-pound guns mounted on the flat roof and were designed to have a garrison of twenty-four gunners.

Originally, twenty such buildings were planned in Suffolk along with two large eight-gun towers. These structures were to be placed at strategic locations along the coast between Felixstowe in the south and Aldeburgh in the north. They were designed to repel Napoleon and his armies. Work began in 1809 and eventually seventeen Martello towers were completed with ten associated batteries. The cost of each structure ran to some £3,000. All of the towers except one had three guns (the batteries either had three, four or seven). The last, at Slaughden near Aldeburgh at the entrance to the estuary of the River Alde, was of a unique quatrefoil design, capable of holding four guns.

Of course, Napoleon never invaded and so these odd-looking constructions were never used. Some have been turned into quirky residences. Others just stand defiantly looking out to sea, reminding us of a threat long since passed.

۞

There seems to be three public houses in Suffolk called 'The Case is Altered' which is surprisingly enough not an uncommon name for pubs elsewhere in the country. But what is curious about these three are the wildly differing explanations for their names.

The Ipswich pub name is said to date from the Napoleonic Wars when troops were housed in Woodbridge Road, Ipswich. An inn was therefore built nearby to accommodate the soldiers' drinking needs. After the conflict was over and the barracks removed, 'the case was altered' as far as the livelihood of the publican was concerned. An alternative, related explanation is that soldiers returning from the Peninsular War had often occupied a house on a hill (Casa Alta) and therefore coming home, this 'home from home' was anglicised to 'The Case is Altered'.

The Woodbridge pub of the same name, however, has a very different story to tell. One local historian has suggested that the inn stands on a site once occupied by a nunnery. Before the Reformation, a local priest, Father Casey, used to visit the nunnery to hear confession. Soon after the nunnery disappeared, an inn was built on the spot where Father Casey's altar had been, inevitably lending itself to a garbled version of 'Casey's Altar' over the centuries. Sadly, although this is a lovely story, there appears to be no evidence at all that there was any kind of religious house on the site. The pub was apparently called 'The Tankard' until 1870 and nobody has offered an explanation as to the change of name.

Suffolk's third 'The Case is Altered' pub is in Bentley and a wonderful local tale has emerged about its odd name. Legend has it that the pub was once held by a genial landlady who was not too fussy about payment for beer, but when she got married, the case was altered! This pub became a community-owned, largely volunteer-run local watering hole in April 2014. It has over 200 owners; some local and some from the other side of the world. In July 2014, the pub was awarded the Plunkett Foundation UK Rural Community Ownership Award for Better Cooperation and continues to win awards.

❧

There is a sandy track leading out of the village of Icklingham intriguingly called Telegraph Road. The lane runs up the northern slope of the valley before climbing to reach one of the highest points in the area – just over 50m above sea level, at Telegraph Plantation. Today there is no trace of the building which once stood here and which gave the area and road its name. The construction was one of a chain of eighteen such buildings, and the only one in Suffolk, which formed a line from London to Yarmouth. It was one link in the chain of telegraph stations constructed in the early nineteenth century as a means to improve communications between the Admiralty in London and its fleets based on the east coast during the Napoleonic Wars. A first chain of telegraph stations had been built between London and Portsmouth at the end of the previous century and, we must assume, had proved successful.

Each relay station – located between 7 and 10 miles apart – housed an ingenious 'shutter' telegraph. It consisted of a large wooden frame fixed to the roof which had six shutters arranged in pairs. Each shutter was about 3ft square and mounted by means of a central pivot. Ropes were then attached to each shutter so that it could be turned from a closed vertical position to an open horizontal one. Using all six shutters, therefore, there was a large number of combinations which could be created which gave a basic code for users. There were enough available combinations for each letter of the alphabet as well as some which had special significance. The beauty of this system was that the crew who manned each station did not have to be able to understand the signals they were sending and therefore, as in Ickingham, it was manned by local men.

The theory was that the first shutter telegraph station in line, set the shutters to create the desired coded message and the next station along the line would see the signal through their telescope and change their shutters to copy the pattern. This happened all

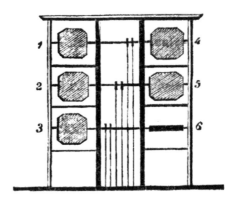

A drawing of the shutter telegraph system.

down the line until the other end was able to read and decipher the message. However, there were obvious disadvantages to such a system. The main problem encountered was poor visibility, usually due to fog.

With the signing of the peace treaty with Napoleon in May 1814, there was no further use for the shutter telegraphs and the whole line of structures, along with the land they stood on, were sold. It is unlikely that any of the buildings survived very long: the Icklingham one appears on a map of 1840 but is nowhere to be seen on the first Ordnance Survey map dating from the 1880s.

०᛫०

There is a rather interesting road which forms part of the boundary between Ipswich and Rushmere. It is called Humber Doucy Lane. Rushmere Heath has had a chequered past, being a battleground for the Danes and Saxons as well as the place where Ipswich hanged its criminals (just over its own borders!). During the Napoleonic Wars, however, the heath was used as a camp for French prisoners of war. These prisoners were said to enjoy the 'ombre douce' or 'sweet shade' of the lane which ran along the heath. After time this phrase turned into the English 'Humber Doucy'.

᪥ NESS ᪥

Orford Ness is a coastal strip of shingle beach some 11 miles long; constantly changing and vulnerable to erosion and extreme weather. It is, perhaps, better known nowadays for the top-secret testing station which was built there in the twentieth century. Now abandoned with only a small museum for visitors, the derelict 'pagodas', designed for rapid collapse in the event of a nuclear attack, give the area a distinctly eerie feel.

Fewer people, however, are aware that Orford Ness played host to a 'miracle' in 1555, often referred to as the Sea Pea Harvest. The story was told by three separate chroniclers, the first being John Caius who contributed to a volume of *Historia Animalium* (History of Animals). In 1558 he wrote:

> On our native British coast peas, which are only seen to the east, at a certain place in Suffolk, between the towns of Aldeburgh and Orford, in the autumn of the year 1555 falling among stones (it was said to be miraculous), with no earth round about, grew of their own accord in such great abundance as to be sufficient even for thousands of people.

Caius does not say whether he actually saw the sea peas himself. Nor are we clear whether William Bullein was an eyewitness. We know, however, that Bullein was rector of nearby Blaxhall from 1550 although he is thought to have already moved out of Suffolk by 1555. He wrote a fuller account seven years after the event:

> In a place called Orford, in Suffolk, stones between the haven and the main sea, whereas never plough came, nor natural earth was, but stones only, infinite thousand ships loden in that place. There did pease grow … Very sweet to eat upon, and served many poor people dwelling there at hand which else should have perished for hunger, the scarce [scarcity] of bread that year was so great.

Across the country there had been a particularly poor harvest; the fifth in a row compounded by heavy rainfall. As a result of this and other economic factors, food prices were 60 per cent higher. There were reports of the labouring classes eating acorns and even animal dung during these food shortages. It is hardly surprising then that this prolific crop of sea peas was seen as a miracle. The sea peas could have been boiled to form broth or mixed with grain to make bread. So for many, it could have meant the difference between life and death.

Today, the sea pea is still found on Orford Ness and on similar shingle spits in Britain. So why was the 1555 harvest seen as a miracle? It is simply that the species had not grown there before and was unknown to locals. We do not know how it arrived there but some theories point to a wrecked ship carrying peas and other foodstuffs. What we do know is that the shingle bank was only just forming in the sixteenth century and therefore a suitable habitat for the sea pea had only just appeared.

❧

Ness Point in Lowestoft is the most easterly place in the United Kingdom. It is said that Sir Samuel Morton Peto, who was largely responsible for the development of the town in the early nineteenth century, used to go to Ness Point to mull over his plans. He was reportedly happier knowing that there was nobody further east than he.

However, given this proud boast it is only recently that the authorities have sought to capitalise on this this by making it the focus for exciting new developments in the town. There is still little for tourists to see beyond the bleakness of the situation. Nevertheless at least there is now 'Gulliver', the country's largest wind turbine, which is capable of producing 2.75MW of electricity. That level of production is enough to supply over 1,500 homes with a saving in excess of 6,000 tonnes of greenhouse gas emissions per year. Sadly the only other tourist attraction is the Euroscope: a large, flat plaque on the concrete showing the distance to various other locations such as the most northerly point (Dunnet Head, Caithness, Scotland) which is 465 miles away and the most southerly point in the British Isles, Lizard Point in Cornwall which lies 352 miles away.

This particular part of Lowestoft is now undergoing a massive redevelopment programme with the ObisEnergy centre at its heart. It is hoped this will become a major centre for renewable energy by providing office accommodation, and meeting and conference facilities for suppliers, large utility companies and small- and medium-sized businesses.

❧

In 2003, the village of Thorpeness on the Suffolk coast just north of Aldeburgh was voted the weirdest village in England by *Bizarre* magazine. Whether or not the thousands of visitors who flock there every year agree with this statement, I am sure they would all say that it was a unique experience.

Although there was originally a small fishing hamlet on this spot called Thorpe, the village of Thorpeness was created only a century ago. In 1910, a Scottish barrister called Glencairn Stuart Ogilvie bought up the whole area

The Meare at Thorpeness. (Tony Scheuregger)

north of Aldeburgh up past Sizewell and inland to Aldringham and Leiston. Most of the land was used for farming. But he was a man with a dream. That vision was to create a private fantasy holiday village to which he would invite his friends and their families.

The whole of Thorpeness was designed by Ogilvie himself, the buildings having a mock Tudor or Jacobean style. He wanted to recreate the age of 'Merrie England' which was all the rage in the Edwardian era. In the centre of the village, and forming a focus for tourist activity today, is a shallow, artificial boating lake which Ogilvie called the Meare, using the Elizabethan spelling. Here he built an adventure playground with tiny islands named after locations found in J.M. Barrie's *Peter Pan*; the author was a friend. Children are encouraged to land their boats on 'The Pirate's Lair', 'Wendy's House' and 'The Smugglers' Cave' amongst others. The Meare is the location for the annual Thorpeness Regatta in August. Many of the boats are named after the workmen who dug the lake.

The other famous feature of Thorpeness is the House in the Clouds, which was built in 1923 as a water tower. It was disguised as a house with weatherboarding in keeping with the rest of the buildings. In 1977 the five-storey water tower was made redundant when mains water was supplied to the village. It was converted into accommodation and includes sixty-eight steps up to the top of the 70ft tower, which now hosts a fabulous games room.

❧ OSTRICHES ❧

There is a public house in Wherstead, now nestling in the shadow of the twentieth-century Orwell Bridge, called the Oyster Reach. However, in modern times, it has only borne this name since 1995. Oyster beds were once common along this river estuary and oysters had been a popular working-class food; in the fifteenth century oysters were priced at *2d* per hundred, the same price as a couple of plaice. And so it seemed logical that the pub should be renamed the Oyster Reach as it was thought that the name under which it was known since at least the mid-eighteenth century – the Ostrich – was a corruption of the proper name, Oyster Reach. However, this may not be right at all.

It is far more likely that the pub was originally called the Ostrich. One of the early seventeenth-century local landowners was Sir Edward Coke, a prominent Elizabethan and Jacobean barrister, judge and politician. Coke held the estate of nearby Bourn Hall from 1609 and when he acquired the right to bear arms and to have a family crest, he chose the unexpected emblem of the ostrich with a horseshoe in its beak. From early times, it was believed that the ostrich could digest everything, even iron. As a Latin scholar, Coke would have known that the verb *conquere*, which sounded like Coke, meant to both eat and to digest. And so to accompany the ostrich on his coat of arms he devised his personal motto *Prudens qui patiens etenum durissima coquit*, which translates as 'The prudent one is the patient one because he digests the hardest things'. As the ostrich is able to eat the hardest things, so does the patient lawyer who, having absorbed the hardest lessons of the law, bides his time, rides others' misfortunes and survives to fight another day.

❦

In the *Bury and Norwich Post* of 8 October 1788 the following advertisement appears:

> To the ladies. Berrow from London, manufacturer of ostrich feathers, artificial flowers and ladies fans; acquaints the ladies, that he has opened a booth in the Long Row, Bury Fair, with a large assortment of the above articles. N.B. Ostrich Feathers, cleaned, to look like new, on the shortest notice.

This and other local newspapers, during the eighteenth century in particular, are simply littered with such advertisements from all manner of tradesmen selling their wares at the annual Bury Fair.

Known originally as St Matthew's Fair, and dating back as far as 1272, the fair was held on the town's Angel Hill each late September and early October. From early times, traders would descend on Bury to set up their sales booths which attracted the highest levels of society. In the sixteenth century, Mary Tudor, the sister of Henry VIII, came every year from her nearby manor of Westhorpe, having her own luxurious pavilion erected on Angel Hill, where she held court and entertained noble guests. A host of entertainments were put on at the time of the Bury Fair: balls and theatre for the well-to-do and a proliferation of travelling artists, circus acts and freak shows visited to keep the working classes happy.

In 1825, Madame Tussaud brought her collection of waxworks to the fair where it appears to have been the main attraction. And ten years later, one of the fair's highlights was a balloon ascent by the intrepid Mr Green who, by that time, had 209 ascents to his credit.

The *Bury Fly* taking passengers to the Bury Fair in 1750.

However, the Bury Fair was not welcomed by all the locals. As early as 1734, local shopkeepers' concerns that they were losing trade as a result of the fair were reflected in a notice in the *Ipswich Journal* which warned that:

> St Matthew's Fair, which … hath of late years been prolonged and continued from the 18th day of September till the 8th or 9th of October, and sometimes longer … for the future will not be continued longer than the 2nd day of October … and all persons selling goods or wares therein … after that time will be prosecuted.

But it was in 1815 that real bitterness arose between the visiting traders and the local fraternity, which resulted in unsuccessful legal proceedings to try to curtail the fair. But by 1825, the fair was starting to decline. In 1866 a petition was raised for the fair's abolition on the grounds of 'immorality' and the nuisance it caused to residents on Angel Hill. The last Bury Fair was held in 1871.

❖ OX ❖

Any visitor to Suffolk cannot fail to notice the numerous cottages and farmhouses which have their exterior painted pink. The traditional shade of this colour has, indeed, become known as 'Suffolk Pink'. Nowadays most of the major paint manufacturers offer masonry paint in 'Suffolk Pink', thus perpetuating the misconception that there is only one 'right' hue. And even some village plans drawn up by councils stipulate a certain pink colour. But the truth is that before about the 1970s there was probably no standard colour. Indeed, other colours such as lavender and orange were also prevalent.

The other common misconception is that it is the ox or pig blood in the mixture that gives it the distinctive pink colour. In fact, whilst the blood added to the traditional whitewash (known as distemper) probably enhanced the resulting colour, it acted more as a binding agent. The main source of the colour itself came from adding either red ochre or sloe berries.

In the past decade or so, a number of stories have hit both the local and national press about property owners being ordered by the relevant authorities to paint their houses an appropriate shade of pink after recent makeovers. By far the most famous example is that of the dispute between the celebrity chef, Marco Pierre White, and Babergh District Council over the exterior colour of the fifteenth-century Angel Hotel in Lavenham which he owned from 2011 until 2014. There had been complaints after he had repainted it an 'unacceptable' shade of pink which some described as blancmange. Happily a negotiated settlement was reached between the two parties which resulted

The Swan at Lavenham has always been an 'acceptable' colour, unlike its rival, the Angel.
(Tony Scheuregger)

in the famous hotel being painted in a deeper pink colour to match other properties in the village. Since then, however, the new owners have restored it to a previous cream colour, again in keeping with the neighbourhood.

❦

It is likely that very few Suffolk residents can name their county flower. It is, in fact, the oxlip (*primula elatior*) which came top in a poll run by the wild plant conservation charity Plantlife. Although the flower is common in continental Europe, it has very restricted distribution in England where it is found almost exclusively in damp, ancient woodlands on boulder clay. Therefore some of the best sites in the country are found where Suffolk borders Essex and Cambridgeshire. In particular, two of the Suffolk Wildlife Trust's sites – Bradfield Woods and Bull's Wood, Cockfield – host spectacular displays of oxlip, which are at their best in April and May.

Like many other wildflowers, the oxlip has come under threat from loss of habitat. It used to be found in meadows in Suffolk but seems to have disappeared in the nineteenth century. And much of the woodland has been lost either during the Second World War (the land being turned over for agriculture) or during the 1960s when conifers were planted instead. But the greatest current threat is from deer grazing, due to the rapid expansion in the deer population in this region. So given that the oxlip is also slow to colonise, this delicate, yellow flower with its apricot scent is now classified as 'near threatened'.

✤ PERAMBULATIONS ✤

Until the Ordnance Survey started, in the early nineteenth century, to publish large-scale maps showing parish boundaries, it was common practice for groups of parishioners to walk their boundaries marking trees and stones as they went. This tradition was called 'perambulation' or 'beating the bounds' and was usually carried out at Rogationtide (the days leading up to Ascension Day).

Knowledge of the boundaries of each parish was important so that such matters as liability to contribute to the repair of the church, and the right to be buried within the churchyard, were not disputed. The vicar or rector together with the churchwardens and other parish officials led a crowd of boys who, armed with green boughs (usually birch or willow) beat the parish boundary markers with them. Sometimes the boys were themselves whipped or even violently bumped

on the boundary markers to make them
remember. The object of taking boys along was
to ensure that witnesses to the boundaries should
survive as long as possible. The priest would pray
for the parish's protection in the forthcoming year.

Detailed records of these perambulations were
kept, usually in the parish records and, where
they survive, provide a fascinating insight into
this tradition. Among the papers which survive
from the Elmsett parish chest are two small
notebooks which contain long, detailed records
of perambulations covering the period 1733
and 1838, some listing the men and boys who
took part. There appears to have been a particular
dispute with the adjacent parish of Hintlesham
over a field called Cold Acre. And to underline the
importance attached to getting the boundaries
right, there is a piece of paper inserted into the
notebooks which is a testimony from an elderly parishioner which
details his recollections of the Cold Acre field boundaries:

A list of persons who
took part in the parish
perambulation in Rickinghall
Inferior on 17 May 1814.
(Courtesy of the Rector of
Rickinghall Inferior)

> May 31 1740
>
> The Deposition of Edward Abbot, born in the Parish of Elmsett in Suffolk
>
> This Deponent saith that he is about 80 years old; and that he lived eleven years
> with Mr Crane, before Mr Coe, and went the Bounds of the said parish every year
> with Mr Crane. And he saith that the Bounds thro' Cold Acre lye from an Oak as
> you enter the field from the road, to another Old Markd Oak in the lower end
> of the said field; and he further says that he remembers another markd oak which
> stood in the said field about six years from the fence belonging to Gawing; and that
> there is not above half an acre of Cold Acre field that lies in the next parish; all the
> other part of the said field lying in the parish of Elmsett aforesaid. All this he is ready
> to attest upon oath; and has set his mark to what he has here deposed.

Sadly any papers which the Hintlesham parish officers may have kept on their
own perambulations do not survive. Nor do we know whether there was any
related legal dispute between the two villages.

☙❧

We are lucky that papers survive which document a rather absurd boundary dispute between the Suffolk parishes of Eye and Wortham dating from 1830. The argument itself was over a very common issue in those days which related to the legal place of settlement of an individual. The Poor Law Act of 1601 had made the parish officers responsible for providing for paupers in their community, although only those people who could prove that they had a legal right to live in that parish. As a result of these laws, parishes frequently argued with one another in the courts if there was some doubt over where a particular person was deemed to be settled. The aim for the Overseers of the Poor in the parish was, of course, to prove that a pauper was not legally entitled to live there and therefore not liable to poor relief.

The pauper in question was 38-year-old Thomas Woods who had served in the army but who had returned from service some twelve years previously with an eye condition which had since ended in blindness. Thomas had lived in Eye since his return which was where he had been born. However, the Overseers of the Poor in Eye tried to argue that this pauper was not legally settled in the parish because he had previously lived in Wortham before enlisting. Starting at the age of 13, Thomas Woods had worked for just over a year with a Mr Hammond who was the landlord of a pub then called the Burgate Dolphin which actually sat on the boundary of Burgate and Wortham. Thomas had lived in the pub, sleeping in a bedroom above the kitchen. The extremely detailed brief written by the parish officers in Wortham for their solicitor explains that their opposite numbers in Eye were saying that although the bed in which Thomas slept lay in both the parishes of Wortham and Burgate, his head lay in Wortham and therefore he should be deemed to have been settled in Wortham. However, the Wortham Overseers of the Poor contended that since Thomas lay in both parishes when asleep at night, then he cannot be deemed to have been settled in either parish, and therefore was still legally resident in the parish of his birth, Eye. Wortham's argument was supported by evidence of perambulations made by the parish of Burgate which were outlined in the lawyer's brief:

It appears that they, on these occasions, entered at the front door opening into the Kitchen and proceeded in a straight line to and entered the Washhouse (a sort of lean-to erected within a few years) where they put a stick thro' a hole at the right hand corner of the Washhouse – that they then returned into the Kitchen; and going out at the back door went round by the Washhouse, taking a circle at the back of the house returned to the back door and again went out at the front. The track thus taken is distinguished by a dotted line in the plan. The front door and the door of the Washhouse are opposite each other and supposing the boundary line to run in the centre of the space between these doors and supposing (which appears to be the fact) that all that part of the house on the right of this line lies in the Parish of Burgate it will follow that the room in which the pauper slept is wholly in that Parish and that therefore the settlement is in Burgate.

It would seem from this description, therefore, that Wortham was in the clear. But the brief continues to explain that there is a suggestion now that some of the bedroom in which Thomas slept was, in fact, in Wortham, especially the part of the room where the head of the bed was positioned. It would be wonderful to know what took place in court, and how some of these ridiculous arguments played out. However, no record of the legal proceedings survives. All we have is a short announcement in the *Ipswich Journal* of 17 July 1830 which says: 'Ipswich Quarter Sessions: Wortham appellants and Eye respondents; orders quashed on debate.' And so Thomas Woods, the blind ex-soldier, was allowed to settle where he had wanted to: in the parish of Eye.

⊰ PIRATES ⊱

According to any self-respecting local history book on the market town of Haverhill, its origins are lost in the mists of time, although it was mentioned in the Domesday Book compiled in 1086. Such histories then continue to explain that the town was probably first settled permanently around the beginning of the eleventh century, the place name 'Haver' meaning 'barley', pointing to a grain-growing district. However, an article printed in the *Haverhill Echo* sometime in 1971 suggests a rather more interesting origin of the town's name:

Today Haverhill's future depends on the movement of people from the London area to our town. Over 1,000 years ago the movement was in the opposite direction, from Haverhill to London. This movement was led by a rascally pirate, Haver, from which Haverhill derives its name.

No other man connected with the town has ever had so much power. From a marauding Danish pirate Haver rose to conquer much of England and even defeat the noble Alfred the Great in battle.

Haver was the son of one of the greatest Danish warriors, Ragnor Lodbrok, and his Norwegian wife. His real name was Hjalmar but because of his mixed parentage the Danes nicknamed him Halfdane or Halver. When he arrived in England the men fighting him soon corrupted Halver to Haver, which meant he-goat, because of his beard and helmet.

Haver came to England for the first time in AD 850 with his father and brothers on a scavenging expedition, raiding a few coastal settlements and looting. He continued terrorising the coast for about fifteen years until in AD 866 he settled in East Anglia and made peace with the people. After supplying himself and his relations from the land, Haver moved north and conquered Northumberland, his father being killed in the fighting. Returning south he found the East Anglians had grown tired of their unwelcome visitors and had to fight to regain his position, killing King Edmund, now immortalised in Bury St Edmunds, in AD 869.

It was about this time that he came to our town and built an outpost here. Never satisfied with his gains, Haver planned further plunder and conquests. Convincing his enemies that he was leaving England, Haver and his warriors sailed away into the North Sea, and then doubled back and along the Thames. Before anyone knew what happened he arrived at Reading. After a series of savage attacks Haver had conquered Wessex and Alfred was forced to sue for peace.

Haver was now virtual ruler of much of England and settled himself for a short while at London where he had coins bearing his name and head minted. Unfortunately our Haver was never satisfied and in AD 879 the lure of rich monasteries for plunder drew him back to Ireland where his fleet came unstuck in the Strangford Loch near Belfast, and Haver was drowned.

The Danish pirate Haver – more commonly known as Ivar the Boneless – certainly did exist according to Norse legend, being one of four sons of Ragnar

A fifteenth-century illustration showing the 'Great Heathen Army' in England.

Lodbrok. Ivar is also 'credited' with being one of the leaders of the 'Great Heathen Army' who defeated the East Anglian army and killed King Edmund. Sadly, his links to Haverhill are less certain, although it does make for a more romantic explanation for the town's name.

◦ϒ◦

When we think of pirates, we naturally imagine the swashbuckling adventurers with ships sporting the Jolly Roger. And although piracy was predominantly a male occupation, there have been a few notable female pirates. Two of the most famous women pirates of the sixteenth century were from Suffolk.

Lady Mary Killigrew clearly had piracy running through her blood. Born sometime around 1525, she was the daughter of Philip Wolverston of Woolverstone Hall (often described as a 'gentleman pirate'). Lady Mary's second husband was Sir John Killigrew who came from an ancient Cornish family who were themselves infamous for their piratical activities all along the south-west coastline. The Killigrews' Cornish home, Arwenack House, was fortified like a stronghold and was regularly used to store merchandise stolen in raids on ships. Mary and her husband paid large fees to officials, bribing them to allow their illicit activities. Mary played an active role in the piracy, and apparently enjoyed the adventure more than her husband. Although piracy was, to a certain extent, tolerated by Queen Elizabeth I, it was still a dangerous occupation to follow. However, in 1582 Mary and her husband were arrested for receiving stolen goods from the Spanish ship *Marie of San Sebastian* which had been anchored opposite Arwenack House. Mary was found guilty and sentenced to death. Although two of her accomplices were executed, Queen Elizabeth pardoned Lady Mary Killigrew, aware that her family may prove useful allies in the future. Despite this serious brush with the law, it is likely that Mary continued her piracy albeit keeping a lower profile.

Another Suffolk woman also aided and abetted her pirate husband, by all accounts relishing the excitement. Margery Lambert's husband Peter was a pirate in Aldeburgh. Official records tell us that the piracy commissioners in Suffolk were informed in December 1577 that Margery had received stolen goods from Peter Lambert in the form of eighteen yards of cloth as well as a taffeta hat and cap. She clearly escaped arrest, although her husband was not so lucky. Peter was imprisoned on charges of piracy and whilst in Aldeburgh jail was visited by his wife. Margery had apparently baked a pie to take to him and in it she had secreted a file. Peter then sawed through the bars of his cell and escaped to sea, taking his enterprising wife with him.

✥ QUAKE ✥

Soon after nine on the morning of Tuesday April 22nd of last year, the eastern parts of this country were shaken by a seismic disturbance, which, although happily unattended by loss of life, for destructiveness and wide distribution has been without parallel in Britain for at least four centuries.

So starts the *Report on the East Anglian Earthquake of April 22nd 1884* co-authored by a professor of chemistry and an eminent geologist. The volume continues to record the effects of the earthquake and damage sustained. Much of this evidence comes from individuals in various locations across the region and contains some fascinating, minute detail of how it impacted on those who experienced it.

Although Essex was the worst hit by the quake as Colchester was the epicentre, the whole county of Suffolk seems to have felt the shock. From measurements taken in 1884, we now know that the quake measured 4.6 on the Richter scale (which was developed in the 1930s). The effects were felt across England as well as in northern France and Belgium. Although not the largest in terms of magnitude, the destruction it wrought was large, including the destruction of over 1,200 buildings.

Many of the correspondents with the report's authors reported rumbling, shaking of furniture and walls, and bells being rung. The Rector of Barham reports:

The earthquake was felt at 9.18, or it began a few seconds earlier. Watch tested by railway clock set by Greenwich time-signal the same day. It seemed like the passing of one wave S to N or SSW to NNE. Rumbling noise preceded. Rattling of windows followed, as though by several shorter undulations. Bells rang in neighbouring houses. Duration about 6 to 8 seconds … the movement distinctly elevated the chair upon which I sat and moved it just as a boat upon an otherwise calm sea would be moved by a solitary wave passing underneath it. In the bedrooms the crockery rattled, as did the windows for some seconds after the chief movement of the earth had passed.

The *Ipswich Journal* of 26 April 1884 carried many eyewitness accounts of the effects of the earthquake. One person reported:

I was sitting reading in an easy chair in the dining room, when I heard a sharp rumbling noise, which I took at first for the passing of the Royal Artillery. Instantly, however, I felt an unusual rocking sensation – rather pleasing than otherwise – my chair appearing to rise up and down … Curiously enough, the shock was felt by our neighbours on one side but not on the other. A lady in an adjoining house had a distinct feeling of nausea, induced by the unusual sensation.

The newspaper's editorial wisely concludes:

It is a matter for congratulation that whilst Tuesday's shock caused somewhat widespread damage of a minor sort, it was not a terrible calamity. We have however no reason to complain, having experienced that which in England will be recorded as a first class earthquake, and one which will hand us down to posterity as the survivors of an alarming catastrophe.

☙❦❧

The county of Suffolk has a long history of religious dissent, stretching back to the late fourteenth century. But after around 1600, nonconformity grew rapidly. In Suffolk the two most important denominations were the Quakers who saw no need for a ministry between the believer and God, and the Independents (or Congregationalists) who believed that each congregation should be self-governing. The seventeenth century saw several periods during which nonconformists were persecuted for their faith but in 1672, Charles II allowed official licensing of nonconformist ministers and places of worship (usually private houses). We know, therefore, that there were at least ninety-eight towns and villages in Suffolk which contained nonconformist congregations at that time, with twenty-seven having more than one. Quaker meetings were not licensed and by nature of their organisation, a monthly meeting would rotate among several venues, but we know that there were forty-two Quaker meetings in the county in the 1670s.

William and Mary passed the 1689 Toleration Act which recognised fully all religious dissenters.

Final recognition of religious dissenters came in 1689 with the Toleration Act under King William III and Queen Mary II. This is when many purpose-built chapels were erected by various denominations. On 19 August 1689, Halesworth's Independent congregation were granted the lease of a sixteenth-century farmhouse in Walpole at an annual rent of 10s. The farmhouse was transformed into a dramatically large, full-height room with box pews downstairs and a tiered gallery above on three sides of the building, all facing a hexagonal canopied pulpit from which the minister would conduct the service. Today, it is one of the oldest nonconformist chapels in England and although it is now formally closed, it continued as a regular place of worship through to 1970. It is now maintained by a national body called the Historic Chapels Trust.

⊹ QUEENS ⊹

Like many other counties, Suffolk can boast many royal links. But perhaps others can't quite match an intriguing link to Anne Boleyn. As any self-respecting schoolboy or girl can tell us, Anne was the second of Henry VIII's six wives, and was the first to be beheaded. Her family roots were in East Anglia: the Boleyns had owned and lived in Blickling Hall in Norfolk until around the time of Anne's birth. And she apparently spent time at Erwarton Hall on the Shotley Peninsula, the home of her aunt and uncle.

Anne Boleyn died on 19 May 1536 in a private execution at the Tower of London. Her ladies-in-waiting took her body and prepared it for burial in the royal chapel of St Peter ad Vincula. It is at this point that a legend kicks in. It is said that Anne's heart was removed from the body and, according to one of her last wishes, it was buried in the church at Erwarton. That said, there are other places in the east who lay claim to her heart, namely Salle in Norfolk and Horndon-on-the-Hill, Essex. Although the practice of heart burial had been common in the fourteenth century, it had all but died out in the next. Nevertheless it is possible that it did happen.

Even more curious is that Erwarton appears to have a distinct edge over its competitors for this particular honour. It is recorded that in 1838, during renovations in the church, a heart-shaped leaden box covered with lime was discovered walled into an alcove. Eyewitnesses told of the moment when the box was opened: inside was only a little black dust. The box was reburied beneath the organ with a small plaque marking the spot.

The local pub which was open until 2009, used to be called the Erwarton Queen's Head, the sign sporting a portrait of Anne Boleyn – an apt name given the manner in which she died. However, I feel they missed a trick, as I don't believe there is another such establishment in the country called the Queen's Heart.

๑๖

When Henry VIII met Anne of Cleves, his fourth bride-to-be, in January 1540 (sadly too late to back out of the betrothal) he is reported to have said, 'I like her not!' He was apparently duped into marrying her by an unrealistically flattering portrait of her crafted by his court painter, Hans Holbein. As a result, the marriage lasted a mere six months before it was annulled. However, Anne was a shrewd operator and negotiated a generous settlement including a castle, a royal palace and several other large estates. One of these was in Haverhill where the parsonage, lands and right to appoint clergy were granted to her.

The sixteenth-century Anne of Cleves House in Haverhill is said to have been her house in the town. However, it is highly likely that it only gained this name in the 1960s when an enterprising estate agent was marketing the property. The majority of dwellings in Haverhill were burned to the ground in 1667 when a devastating fire swept through the town and it is probable that her original house perished in the flames.

๑๖

As far as Tudor celebrities in Suffolk go, they didn't get much more important than the former Queen of France and her husband. Mary Tudor (also known by some as Mary Rose) was Henry VIII's sister who had been married to King Louis XII of France until his death in 1515. She had then married (in secret and against her brother's wishes) Charles Brandon, who was a close friend of the king. When Henry VIII calmed down, he made Brandon the Duke of Suffolk. Eventually, the Duke and Duchess of Suffolk settled in Westhorpe, rebuilding the existing manor house there. Mary Tudor died at Westhorpe in 1533.

As Dowager Queen of France and sister of the king, Mary Tudor's funeral was a lavish affair. She was to be buried in the abbey church at Bury St Edmunds. For the journey from Westhorpe, her coffin was placed upon a hearse draped in black velvet embroidered with Mary's arms and her motto 'The will of God is sufficient for me'. The coffin was covered in a pall of black cloth edged with gold, and on top of this was an effigy of Mary wearing robes of state, a crown

Mary Tudor's final resting place in St Mary's church, Bury St Edmunds. (Tony Scheuregger)

on her head and a golden sceptre which signified Mary's status as Dowager Queen of France. The hearse was drawn by six horses wearing black cloth and the coffin was covered by a canopy carried by four of Suffolk's knights. Surrounding the coffin, standard bearers carried the arms of the Brandon and Tudor families. At the head of the procession walked one hundred torch bearers who comprised members of the local community who were paid and dressed in black for the funeral. Next came members of the clergy who carried the cross. After them came the household staff followed by the six horses pulling the hearse. Behind the hearse came the knights and other noble men in attendance followed by one hundred of the duke's yeomen. Lastly came Mary's daughter Frances, the chief mourner, and other ladies. Along the way, the funeral procession was joined by members of the local parishes. Mary Tudor was finally laid to rest in the abbey.

Ordinarily, this may have been the end of the story, were it not for the fact that Mary's brother, the king, dissolved the abbey along with similar institutions across the country. And so merely six years after her interment in the abbey church, Mary Tudor's body was removed and reburied in the nearby St Mary's church. In 1784 her remains were disturbed again when her altar monument was removed because it obstructed the approach to the rails of the communion table. Her resting place is now marked by a slab on the floor and plaques on the wall above.

❖ REMOVALS ❖

When we talk of moving house, it usually conjures up in our minds packing cases, removal vans and 'For Sale' signs. However, in 1972 the most remarkable case of moving house took place on the outskirts of Sudbury. And although there have been many similar removals recorded before and after this one, it was certainly one of the most dramatic.

Ballingdon Hall is a sixteenth-century house built by Sir Thomas Eden, a prosperous Sudbury citizen. Originally constructed in a typical Elizabethan H-shape with an oak frame, the house which remains today has two storeys, attics and cellars, comprising a total of twenty-five rooms. We also know that it weighed 170 tonnes. Not something you usually get to know about your house! But in this case it was crucial. In 1972 the owners of Ballingdon Hall decided on a rather drastic course of action. They could no longer enjoy an uninterrupted view of the River Stour valley due to the construction of a

housing estate in front of their
property and improvements
to the main road running
past the estate. They therefore
engaged contractors to move
the house to another site on
their land 1,000 yards away and
some 50ft higher up the hill.

To enable the contractors to
move the hall without dismantling it,
the hall was released from its

Ballingdon Hall on the move in 1972.
(Courtesy of Sudbury Museum Trust)

foundations and interior brickwork was removed to lighten the load. It was
then winched onto a steel frame supported by twenty-six large wheels and
slowly hauled up the hill. This removal became the most photographed
1,000 yards in history and caused traffic jams in the local area. During the
fifty-two days it took to move the house, it is estimated that 50,000 people
visited the site to watch the spectacle. They were charged 10 pence each and
all the proceeds were donated to All Saints church in Sudbury. The family were
able to move back into Ballingdon Hall in 1975. It is estimated that the cost
of the move was in the region of £80,000 but clearly a small price to pay for
continued enjoyment of the view over the valley and for the owner's privacy.

☙❧

Removals do not always involve houses. In 1850, Charles May, one of the
partners of Ransomes of Ipswich, bought a fully grown tree from a fellow
resident. He therefore needed to move the tree the distance of about a mile
from the garden in London Road to his own home in Bolton Lane. When
the tree and its roots had been extracted from the ground it was somehow
levered over the wall of the garden and on to a wagon drawn by five horses.
After its journey the tree was similarly manoeuvred into a waiting hole in
Mr May's garden. His father wrote in a letter shortly after the move that it was
'accomplished without any accident except breaking a window or two … it is
planted in sight of the dining room window and will look very nice if it grows.'
The Mays moved away from Ipswich the following year and so were never able
to benefit from their remarkable tree.

☙❧

The Magpie Inn in Stonham Parva sits on the now busy A140 which runs from Norwich down to meet the A14 near Ipswich. The road has always been a major route through the region and so clearly a good place to have a public house. We don't know exactly when the fifteenth-century house was first used as an inn but we do know that until the late nineteenth century it was called the 'Pye' or 'Pie'. Magpie is an old term for a half pint, and so would be a good name for a drinking establishment. Until the twentieth century it had a live magpie in a cage on the exterior wall which acted as a living pub sign. The Magpie is one of a handful of inns left in Britain which has a 'gallows'-style sign spanning the road with a magpie as its centrepiece. In the 1970s a tiny thatched house called Mustard Pot Cottage was moved from Mendlesham to the outskirts of Needham Market, along the A140. The Magpie Inn's sign across the road had to be temporarily removed to accommodate the cottage's passage.

❖ RIOT ❖

Medieval Bury St Edmunds was so prone to rioting that it has recently been dubbed the Brixton of the fourteenth century. There were many well-documented riots in the time of the abbey when tensions rose between the abbot and the townspeople. But even long after the Dissolution of the Monasteries, the town was the scene of uprisings. One such occurrence was during the period of the Civil Wars and the 'Commonwealth' under Oliver Cromwell.

A seventeenth-century woodcut of people dancing round a maypole.

The Puritan parliament had outlawed ritual or religious celebrations, including Christmas. Another casualty of this was May Day, where the tradition of erecting and dancing around a maypole was banned. However, in 1647 a group of townspeople led by Colonel Blague, a staunch Royalist, rebelled against this ruling. They put up a maypole in the Market Square and prepared to dance. The town elders, in an attempt to uphold the law, ordered that it be taken down. A riot ensued and Cromwell's New Model Army of Roundheads were called to deal with the demonstrators.

There have been many causes of riots over the centuries in Suffolk. And they have been spread across the county. But the small hamlet of Bulcamp near Blythburgh is rather unusual in that it saw two separate rebellions, seventy years apart, centered on the same institution.

Until 1834, assistance to paupers in England was the responsibility of the parish officers in the place in which the poor person was legally resident. In 1764, the forty-nine parishes which comprised the Blything Union agreed to construct a House of Industry for the poor of their parishes. The chosen site was Bulcamp and construction began in March 1765. It meant that on completion, instead of staying in their own villages and receiving 'outdoor relief' in the form of food, clothing and heating fuel, paupers would be required to live in the new workhouse and to work on tasks within its confines. Families threatened with this fate were therefore concerned that the new building would offer the same appalling conditions for inmates as the existing parish poorhouses.

The *London Magazine* of 5 August 1765 reported that 'on this day and the Monday evening, some thousand persons assembled near Saxmundham and Yoxford, and destroyed a building called the Industry House.' The damage was estimated at over £500. The riot ended badly when soldiers were sent from Ipswich to quell the demonstrators. One man died and six were arrested.

Fears were finally allayed and the building was completed in October 1766. By the following April it had 253 inmates. With the riot in mind, the directors of the House of Industry explained to potential occupants that the conditions would be humane. This would include separate bedrooms for married couples, care of the sick, children to be taught to read, and good new feather beds with proper furniture would be provided.

However, this period of calm was not to last long. In 1832, there was growing dissatisfaction with the whole poor law administration in the country, particularly from the land and property-owning classes who bore the brunt of the poor-rate burden. This led to a review of the system of administering poor relief. The resulting Poor Law Amendment Act meant that from July 1835, families were now required to be split up into different parts of the workhouse. This led to further demonstrations in Bulcamp and on 21 December 1835 it was noted in the Minute Book that 'it having been reported to the Guardians present that a considerable body of men, armed with pickaxes, crowbars, and other implements of destruction were advancing in different directions to attack the Workhouse and the Committee there.' The mob of 200 protestors were not to be persuaded to disperse peacefully and eventually they were dealt with by soldiers from Halesworth and Ipswich. For many months after there were small incidents such as windows being broken, but no further full-scale riots took place.

⊙֊⊚

We have all heard of the expression to 'read the riot act' when some sort of trouble is afoot. The origins of this phrase are quite simple in that a Riot Act was passed by Parliament in 1714. This legislation, which was called in full 'An Act for preventing tumults and riotous assemblies, and for the more speedy and effectual punishing the rioters', gave local authorities the power to declare a gathering of twelve or more people illegal. This meant that such a group would either have to disperse or face arrest. The act provided for standard wording that had to be read out to the assembled gathering which was as follows:

The men of Glemsford were read the Riot Act in 1885. (Tony Scheuregger)

Our Sovereign Lord the King chargeth and commandeth all persons, being assembled, immediately to disperse themselves, and peaceably to depart to their habitations, or to their lawful business, upon the pains contained in the act made in the first year of King George, for preventing tumults and riotous assemblies. God Save The King.

In the early days of the act, it was used to good effect up and down the country but it eventually drifted into disuse. The last time it was read was in 1919 in Birkenhead.

In Suffolk, the last time the Riot Act was read was to the men of the village of Glemsford. This occurred at the time of the first 'working man's election' in 1885 when the new voters of Glemsford were prevented by their 'betters' from casting their votes in the village through the measure of not providing a polling station. This meant that those who wanted to exercise their new democratic right had to walk to the polling station in the neighbouring village of Long Melford, thus losing wages because of the time they had to take off work. The Glemsford men were, however, keen to vote and so marched together to Long Melford where they looted businesses and terrorised the locals. Troops from the garrison at Bury St Edmunds were summoned to provide assistance. When they finally arrived on the train, the Riot Act was read and the rioters dispersed.

❧ SMUGGLING ❧

Smuggling was one of the major crimes which occupied column space in the eighteenth-century newspapers. This illegal trade along England's coast had grown at a prodigious rate. It became a large and lucrative industry despite the penalties imposed for those who were caught in the act. This illicit dealing in perishable goods such as tea, coffee, gin and brandy came about as a direct result of the imposition of crippling taxation by successive governments desperate to fund costly wars in Europe.

It is hardly surprising that Suffolk, with its long coastline, was a major centre for smuggling. Not only did it provide numerous places along the shoreline for landing the illegal imports, it also offered excellent roads from the coast inland capable of taking heavy wagons laden with goods. The Roman road leading towards Stowmarket from the coast was a convenient and well-used route for contraband heading inland. Its progress was only sporadically interrupted by the customs authorities, but nevertheless the passing carts did not go unnoticed. Earl Soham on this route was the home of William Goodwin, a surgeon.

Goodwin lived at Street Farm in the second half of the eighteenth century and the early years of the nineteenth. During this time he meticulously recorded, in his notes entitled *Miscellany of Occurrences Persons and Curiosities was began in the Year 1785 by Wm. Goodwin of Earl Soham Surgeon and is intended as an Universal repository and Chronology,* contraband passing through the village. In the summer of 1785 he noted that, in less than a week, twenty carts had passed by carrying 2,500 gallons of spirits. In February of the same year, five carts carrying 600 gallons passed in the course of just one morning.

Earl Soham was not the only village which the smuggling trade touched. In Monewden, the sexton of the local church was in league with the smugglers, and in February 1790 the revenue services seized nine tubs of spirits that he had hidden behind the Ten Commandments in the church. And the vicar, sexton and clerk at nearby Rishangles were also reputed to be involved in the trade. Indeed these rumours may well have some credence because repairs to the church in the mid-nineteenth century led to the discovery under the pulpit of the remains of kegs and bottles.

⚜

Consuming smuggled goods – whether knowingly or unknowingly – was clearly a hazardous business, as this item from the *Ipswich Journal* of 25 October 1783 illustrates:

> Early on Tuesday afternoon died, in great agony, after breakfasting on her usual Bohea tea, Mrs Simpson, of Shotley, in this county. Mr. S., her husband, was very ill for several hours from the same drink, but recovered; a boy about 14 years of age, and 4 servants were sick after drinking some of the same infusion, one of the latter narrowly escap'd the fate of her mistress. The teapot was, unfortunately, emptied before the arrival of the physician and surgeon. These gentlemen took the canister with them on their return to this town, and have since, with other gentlemen, drank of an infusion from the same tea without any ill effects from it.

An inquest was held into Mrs Simpson's death which was reported in the same newspaper on 1 November 1783. The verdict was that she had died accidentally from a quantity of tea taken 'of some poisonous quality'. To this was added the following:

> The rest of the family are perfectly recovered, and the above melancholy accident should caution persons against making use of smuggled tea, as it is well known that

the hawkers of that article frequently make use of a very pernicious drug, in order to give the tea a finer colour, and if unskilfully made use of, may, as in the above instance, prove fatal.

❧

Despite the high rewards for those brave enough to take on the authorities and engage in smuggling, the occupation was not without its perils. The *Ipswich Journal* of 27 June 1778 reported on an inquest held at Leiston on a pair of

The grave of smugglers Robert Debney and William Cooper in Tunstall churchyard.
(Tony Scheuregger)

young men, Robert Debney and William Cooper, who had entered a cave used as a repository for smuggled goods. The coroner concluded that they had died from asphyxiation from the fumes coming from horse manure which had been laid by the local smugglers to deter excise men. Their gravestone in Tunstall churchyard reads:

All you, dear Friends that look upon this Stone,
Oh! think how quickly both their Lives were gone.
Neither Age, nor Sickness brought them to Clay;
Death quickly took their Strength and Sense away.
Both in the Prime of Life they lost their breath,
And in a Sudden were cast down by Death.
A cruel Death that could no longer spare
A loving Husband nor a Child most dear.
The loss is Great to those they left behind,
But they thro' Christ, 'tis hop'd, True Joys will find.

Some smugglers, however, lived to tell the tale into old age. Sudbourne was the home of a particularly shameless smuggler. On his retirement, he placed this advertisement in a local newspaper:

Richard Chaplin, Sudbourn, Suffolk, near Orford, begs to acquaint his friends and the public in general that he has some time back declined the branch of smuggling and returns thanks for all their past favours. To be SOLD on Monday August 6th at the dwelling house of Samuel Bathers, Sudbourn, the property of Richard Chaplin aforesaid. A very useful Cart fit for a maltster, ashman or smuggler — it will carry 80 half ankers or tubs — one small ditto that will carry 40 tubs; also very good loaden Saddles, three Pads, Straps, Bridles, Girths, Horse-cloth, Corn-bin, very good Vault and many articles that are useful to a smuggler.

⚜ SWIMMING ⚜

In the seventeenth century, East Anglia and, in particular, Suffolk became synonymous with witch hunts, to a large degree because of the presence of the self-styled 'Witchfinder General' Matthew Hopkins. He was brought in by local parishes to find and try any suspected witches. And since he operated on a system of payment by results, it was clearly in his interests to obtain confessions.

The largest single witch trial in England took place in Bury St Edmunds in 1645 when eighteen people were subsequently executed by hanging.

Although simple torture was an effective means of securing a confession, other methods were used, including the pricking of the suspect with needles. It was believed that a witch or wizard would neither feel pain nor bleed. Another popular method was that of 'swimming'. The idea behind this was that it was thought that water rejected servants of the Devil. In 1653, Sir Robert Filmer described how the suspect would be stripped naked and then tied up; the right thumb to the left big toe and vice versa. In this position they would then be secured by ropes and thrown into a deep stream or pond three times. If they sank (and unfortunately often drowned), they were deemed innocent. However, if they floated then they were guilty. Often men with long poles were employed to push them under the water while others, holding onto the ropes, pulled them up again.

The swimming of witches appears to have been commonplace right the way through the eighteenth century. For example, the Monks Eleigh parish register contains the following entry: 'December 19 1748. Alice, the wife of Thomas Green, labourer, was swam, malicious and evil people having raised an ill-report of her for being a witch.' And this report in the *Ipswich Journal* tells of another such case:

> In July 20th 1776, at Farnham, in Suffolk a poor man suspected of being a wizard was swam in the river Deben in the presence of a great number of spectators who had assembled from different parts of the county of Suffolk on the occasion, he was put upon his watery trial about 7 in the evening with his feet and hands tied but to the surprise of the whole company he sunk to the bottom and had it not been for the assistance of a humane spectator the experiment would have terminated in a manner shockingly to its protectors, mortified and disappointed the company soon dispersed, ashamed of themselves and angry at their own weakness and credulity.

However, the last recorded 'swimming' in Suffolk was in 1825 which was reported both in *The Times* newspaper and in *The Annual Register* for that year. The latter carried a blow-by-blow account of how the unfortunate 67-year-old Isaac Stebbings was accused of overlooking his neighbours with the evil. Combined with a few other odd happenings which would not be explained, and faced with

'Swimming' of a suspected witch in 1615.

accusations by villagers of being a wizard, Stebbings offered to be 'swum' in Grimmer Pond at Wickham Skeith. His ordeal lasted more than an hour, watched by crowds of men, women and children. The spectators, not satisfied by this trial which proved inconclusive, demanded another the following week. Luckily, though, the local clergy and churchwardens stepped in to prevent a reoccurrence of the incident.

⊕⊕

There is a curious tale which has been handed down and, as these things are, embellished over the centuries. It involves a strange catch by fishermen off the Suffolk coast at Orford which happened in the time of Henry II (1154–1216). They caught a mysterious, naked creature with the head, body and limbs of a man. He had hair covering his whole body; short in places although extremely shaggy on his chest, with a long beard.

The villagers took the wild man to the then newly built Orford Castle which was in the hands of Bartholomew de Glanville. There he was held in the dungeons for six months where he was restrained and even tortured. He did, or could, not say a word even when pain was inflicted on him. But he ate any foodstuff put in front of him. He was tested further by taking him down to the harbour and imprisoning him in the sea with a line of nets. After appearing to mock the residents by regularly 'escaping' and then deciding to return to his watery jail, he finally swam under the nets and disappeared into the sea never to return.

Although the original (almost contemporary) account of this incident made no mention of a tail, later versions of the story describe him as a merman. Of course, we will never know the truth about this creature but this tale appears to have encouraged the growth, in the late medieval period, of 'wild man' carvings on baptismal fonts in Suffolk churches.

⊹ TRADITIONS ⊹

There can be no Suffolk tradition or custom more curious than dwile flonking. The earliest documented game of flonking the dwile was played as part of the Beccles Festival of Sport in 1966. The organisers of this event claimed that they had first learned of the game after being shown a parchment document entitled *Ye Olde Book of Suffolk Harvest Rituels,* found in an attic. This is likely to have been a complete fabrication as no other evidence has ever been found to back up their claim that this was a tradition dating back to the Middle Ages. Nevertheless, the name alone is an interesting invention. It is thought that the name dwile comes from the Dutch *dweil* for a mop or knitted floor cloth, and a flonk is probably a corruption of 'flong', the old past tense for fling.

The rules of dwile flonking are complex and the result is, in any case, always contested. Two teams dress as yokels and a referee, or jobanowl (traditionally a dull-witted person), is chosen. It is he who decides which team flonks first, by tossing a sugar beet. The dwile – usually a beermat on the end of a pole – is soaked in a pot of beer. The jobanowl shouts 'Here y'go t'gither!' to start the game. One team forms a circle around the flonker – a member of the opposing side – who stands in the middle with the dwile and beer pot. The team dance around the flonker, a practice known as girting. The flonker dips the dwile in the pot and, circling in the opposite direction to the surrounding team, flings it, in an attempt to hit one. Points are scored for striking the head, body and leg. Every member of the team takes a turn at flonking. Once they have done so, the sides swap over. A full game comprises four snurds, each snurd being one team taking a turn at girting. The team with the most points at the end wins and is awarded a ceremonial pewter gazunder (chamber pot). The jobanowl can add interest and difficulty to the game by randomly switching the direction of rotation. He can also levy drinking penalties on any player found not taking the game seriously enough.

The point-scoring system in a game of flonking the dwile are equally amusing. Three points – a 'wanton' – are given for a direct hit on a girter's head, two points for a body hit (called a 'morther' or 'marther') and one point for a leg hit, called a 'ripple' or 'ripper'. Teams also have to ensure that their members cannot be deemed sober at the end of the game because each participant not adjudged to be drunk has one point deducted.

ॐ

It is generally acknowledged that the Ancient House in Ipswich has the country's finest example of pargeting, which was added to the building in the seventeenth century. And whilst this skilled craft is not unique to Suffolk, this county has probably the strongest tradition of this style. It is essentially the ornamentation of plastered building facades that would otherwise be plain. The name probably derives from the old French verb *pargeter*, which means 'to throw about'.

Pargeting on the Ancient House in Ipswich. (Tony Scheuregger)

At its simplest, pargeting comprises geometric patterns scored into the plaster. But at its most elaborate it can be all manner of people, flowers, plants and other creatures formed in relief on top of the masonry. Popular themes include vines and bunches of grapes, corn-stalks and sheaves, oak leaves and acorns (sometimes depicted with a Green Man) and endless variations of repeating patterns of chevrons, scallops or fantails. The pargeting on Ipswich's Ancient House depicts scenes from the four continents: Australasia and Antarctica had not yet been discovered and the Americas were considered a single continent. And another fine example of this art can be seen on the upper level of the Ancient House Museum in Clare.

Despite the high quality of the workmanship on many of Suffolk's pargeted buildings, it is believed that the practice became popular in the time of Henry VIII, primarily to cover up flaws in the base coat of plasterwork, because of the shortage of quality timber at the time: the monarch had decimated the country's oak forests in order to build his navy.

๑๖

The village of Middleton is the only place in the country where there is a recorded history of the ritual known as the Cutty Wren. In 1994 this custom was revived by the Old Glory Molly Dancers and Musicians after nearly a century of neglect. Molly dancing traditionally only appeared during the depths of winter and is regarded by many people as the East Anglian form of the Morris dance. It is characterised by blackened faces, heavy boots (usually hobnailed) and the presence of a 'Lord' and a 'Lady'; two of the men specially attired respectively as a gentleman and his consort, who lead the dances. The musicians play a variety of instruments, which may include at least one four-stop melodeon in the 'Suffolk key' of C, a concertina, drums, a trombone, a 'tea-chest' bass and a rommelpot (a percussion instrument).

In his book *An Hour-glass on the Run* published in 1959, Allan Jobson recalls a tale his grandfather used to tell of when he was a boy in the mid-nineteenth century. He and others would run around Middleton on St Stephen's Day (26 December), the labourers blackening their faces with soot. They would catch and kill a wren and fasten it in the midst of a mass of holly and ivy to the top of a broomstick. Going from house to house they sang:

> The wren, the wren, the king of all birds,
> St Stephen's day was caught in the furze;
> Although he is little, his family is great
> I pray you good landlady, give us a treat!

The men's 'disguise' of black faces was to save their embarrassment at having to beg for money. In earlier times, the procession may have included fantastic characters such as hobby-horses, fiery dragons and rampant serpents whisking their tails about. The culmination of the procession was the ceremonial burial of the wren, accompanied by dancing.

This wren hunt possibly has its origins in Neolithic times when the Druids were believed to have been able to foresee the future by listening to the song of a captured wren. However, in Europe the wren has long been considered the king of birds and it has been thought extremely unlucky to kill one. Nevertheless, it became a custom in many parts of Britain to catch and kill a wren on St Stephen's Day. This may come from the Elizabethan custom of the Lord of Misrule where everything is turned on its head at Christmastide. Although equally it may be because the wren came to be associated with the underworld because of its ability to creep into dark crevices in rocks, and therefore tied in with the winter solstice.

❖ TREASURE ❖

In 1951 at the Festival of Britain in London, there was a large display about one of the most important finds in British archaeology. But there was no mention of the person who had made the discovery. Today, at least, he is recognised in literature as the person without whom the Sutton Hoo Anglo-Saxon ship burial may never have been found. His name was Basil John Wait Brown, a self-taught archaeologist from Rickinghall.

Basil Brown was from humble farming stock and attended the local elementary school in the late 1800s. He left school at the age of 12 to help on his father's farm, although he continued to study in his spare time. At the time, his real passion was astronomy. A few years after taking over the running of the

Basil Brown outside his garden shed and workshop in Rickinghall.
(Courtesy of the Compton family)

farm on his father's death, Basil Brown published a book, *Astronomical Atlases, Maps and Charts* to some acclaim in the world of astronomy. Not only that, but he was reported to speak four languages. He clearly had exceptional talent.

Basil Brown was also a keen archaeologist, interested mainly in Roman remains. Throughout his life he dug numerous sites in Rickinghall and the surrounding area. He excavated, among other things, Roman kilns at Wattisfield (where the famous Henry Watson's Potteries, founded in 1734, still trades). To make ends meet, Basil took a part-time, casual job with the Ipswich Museum, working with others on excavations across Suffolk. And it is while working here that he came to the attention of Mrs Edith Pretty, a landowner in Sutton Hoo near Woodbridge.

So, on Monday, 20 June 1938, Basil Brown started work for Edith Pretty, investigating four mounds on her estate which she felt sure contained something of interest. Basil's diary entry for that first day records that he was 'rather alarmed' by the size of the mounds but dutifully started digging. After finding three previously plundered burials or cremation burials dating from the sixth or early seventh centuries, he came across an undisturbed wooden ship burial held together with iron rivets. After a break over the winter, Basil returned to Sutton Hoo in May 1939 and continued to unearth the 27m-long ship. And another incredible discovery was made: a burial chamber at the end of a 3m-long shaft. It was at this point that news of these discoveries quickly spread in the archaeological world. Although Basil knew that he needed expert assistance in continuing with the dig, he did not realise that he would be sidelined once these reinforcements arrived. Charles Phillips, a Fellow of Selwyn College, Cambridge, and his team were engaged by the Office of Works and completed the excavation. This yielded a whole host of treasures including the iconic iron warrior's helmet. The whole collection from Sutton Hoo is now in a purpose-built gallery in the British Museum.

After the Second World War, Basil Brown continued his archaeological work. He also revelled in passing his knowledge and enthusiasm for digs on to others, especially local children. Over time, Basil Brown's key role in the discovery at Sutton Hoo was finally acknowledged and his story has now been told many times. He made an immense contribution to the development of Suffolk archaeology and, until his death in March 1977 at the age of 89, he was deservedly proud of his find. He is commemorated in Rickinghall Inferior church by a Roman Samian-ware plaque depicting Basil Brown in front of his burial ship discovery.

❦

Whilst ploughing a field in West Row near Mildenhall in January 1942, farmer Gordon Butcher hit a hard object in the ground and set about investigating it. With the help of a colleague, he uncovered a large hoard of silverware buried in the ground. It consisted of two large serving platters, two small decorated serving plates, a deep fluted bowl, a set of four large decorated bowls, two small decorated bowls, two small pedestalled dishes, a deep flanged bowl with a deep, domed cover, five small round ladles with dolphin-shaped handles, and eight long-handled spoons. Amazingly, the men did not recognise the significance of their find – thinking the objects to be made of pewter – and it was not until four years later that their discovery came to the attention of the authorities.

The 'Mildenhall Treasure' as the collection came to be known has since been accepted by experts as being of first-rate Roman art and craftsmanship, dating from the fourth century. In an inquest in the summer of 1946, the hoard was declared 'treasure trove', that is, a legal owner of the find cannot be identified. The silverware therefore became the property of the Crown and was acquired by the British Museum where it has stayed ever since.

What is interesting is that ten years earlier than Mr Butcher's discovery, a team of archaeologists had excavated a Roman villa only metres away from the field in which the treasure was found. The experts then had sadly not been aware of the local legend in West Row that there was treasure buried in the field once known as Thirtley Green, where Mr Butcher found the hoard. Had they known this story, they may have investigated. So although the prominent Roman family who buried the treasure had never been able to return to the spot and retrieve their possessions, it is clear that someone who knew what they had done passed on the tale to their descendants: the legend was remarkably still alive fifteen centuries later.

✤ U-BOATS ✤

During the First World War, it was evident that the civilian population in Britain had a role to play, sometimes accidental and sometimes not. It was soon after the start of the conflict, in September 1914, that the Royal Navy sustained its first serious losses of the war: three cruisers were sunk by a German U-boat in the North Sea. Two Lowestoft trawlers – the *Coriander* and the *J.G.C.* – were fishing nearby and the two skippers steered their ships to the battle scene and rescued 156 British sailors from the sea. Their gallantry was honoured in a ceremony at Lowestoft Town Hall a month later when rewards of £100 in respect of each trawler were presented by the Admiralty and the two skippers were awarded the Board of Trade's silver medal.

The Lowestoft fishing fleet was soon heavily involved in the war at sea. The German U-boats were sinking many of the trawlers. A common tactic was to come alongside, take the catch of fish, order the crew into their lifeboat and then put a bomb aboard the boat. As a consequence, some of the more enterprising Lowestoft skippers persuaded the Admiralty that some of their fishing vessels – smacks – be secretly armed and operated to decoy enemy submarines. The volunteer crews of these boats – codenamed 'Q-ships' – were not to wear uniforms or reveal their gun until the enemy had been lured within range. They were, however, given naval pay as well as danger money in recognition of the peril into which they were putting themselves. When the U-boat was close enough, the cover was whipped off the gun, the Royal Navy's White Ensign was run up the flagpole, and the crew donned naval caps and armbands so that, if they were captured, they might claim prisoner-of-war status.

The Lowestoft Q-ships continued to operate successfully throughout the war, the crews receiving many commendations. One such trawlerman was Skipper Thomas Crisp. After the boat, the *George Borrow*, which he captained was sunk in August 1915, Thomas was recruited into the Royal Naval Reserve and commanded a Q-ship called HM *Smack I'll Try*. In July 1917, *I'll Try* was renamed the HM *Smack Nelson* to maintain its cover following a successful encounter with an enemy sub. On 15 August whilst fishing off the Lincolnshire coast, a German U-boat, UC63, was spotted on the surface. The U-boat saw the smack and began firing, scoring several hits before the *Nelson*'s gun was in range. Although hopelessly outgunned, the *Nelson* fought back, but its hull was hit below the waterline. A shell hit Thomas Crisp, blowing off half his body, but he continued to direct the crew, ordering confidential papers to be thrown overboard and dictating a message to be sent by the boat's carrier pigeons: 'Nelson being attacked by submarine. Skipper killed. Jim Howe Bank. Send assistance at once.' The crew tried to remove their captain from the sinking smack. He ordered them to throw him overboard rather than slow them down. The crew, however, refused to do so, but were unable to move him and he died in his son's arms a few minutes later.

The *Nelson* smack, one of
Lowestoft's Q-ships.

Crisp's crew escaped in the lifeboat and were later found by a search vessel, thanks to their carrier pigeon 'Red Cock'. Crisp was posthumously awarded the VC for his bravery and self-sacrifice in the face of this 'unequal struggle'.

⁂ UGLY ⁂

Holy Trinity church, Long Melford, is widely acknowledged to be one of the finest examples of a medieval church financed by wealthy local wool merchants. The nave – the main body of the church – is 152.5ft long; the longest of any parish church in England. Although much of the interior and exterior of the large church has been altered over the centuries, many original features have survived. Amongst these are various fifteenth-century stained-glass windows, described by one church expert as 'the best collection of medieval glass in Suffolk'.

One of these early stained-glass panels depicts two women facing each other in prayer. The one on the right is Elizabeth Tilney, Countess of Surrey (grandmother to both Anne Boleyn and Katherine Howard) and the other, on the left, Elizabeth Talbot, the wife of the last Mowbray Duke of Norfolk. By all accounts Elizabeth Talbot appears to have been an attractive woman both in appearance and personality. Nevertheless it is often claimed that this stained-glass image of her provided inspiration for John Tenniel's Ugly Duchess drawings in *Alice's Adventures in Wonderland*. However, it appears equally likely, or perhaps even probable, that he drew on Quenten Massys' sixteenth-century painting entitled *Grotesque Old Woman* which hangs in the National Gallery in London.

Tenniel was an illustrator, graphic humourist and political cartoonist who is now best known for the ninety-two drawings he did for Lewis Carroll's two Alice books. Carroll was a regular reader of *Punch* where Tenniel was chief cartoon artist and admired his work.

◈

It might be rather surprising to learn that Knodishall residents are quite proud of their claim to fame which is to live in the ugliest village in Suffolk. But since beauty is, as they say, in the eye of the beholder we will not seek to defend or uphold this assertion. The parish of Knodishall is not actually one village but two separate residential areas surrounded by common land extending to some 29 acres. These greens and commons are its main features and 'commoners' rights' are still exercised by village folk. Traditionally, therefore, they would be

The stained glass depicting Elizabeth Talbot (left) in Long Melford church.
(Tony Scheuregger)

allowed to have their livestock graze on the common, collect firewood or cut turf for fuel. One of the common areas is called Coldfair Green which is widely said to be the really ugly part! Again, although not wanting to take sides in this argument, St Luke's mission church (no longer used as such) in the hamlet is a green, corrugated tabernacle building such as were built cheaply as kits and erected by locals. There were once thousands of these 'tin tabernacles' in the country and now only a few hundred survive.

⚘ VEILS ⚘

In the past, market day in Suffolk towns and villages naturally involved much buying, selling and trading of commodities, just as they do today. But in the eighteenth and nineteenth centuries it was not uncommon to find men taking their wives to market; not to do the shopping, but to be sold to the highest bidder. We do not really know how widespread this practice was across the whole country but it is probable that it was a working-class type of divorce: they could not afford the legal route. Only a few such sales hit the newspapers and these disappear after the divorce laws were reformed to make them more accessible. Here is a report in the *Ipswich Journal* of 29 October 1789:

> Samuel Balls sold his wife to Abraham Rade in the parish of Blythburgh in this
> county for 1s. A halter was put round her, and she was resigned up to this Abraham
> Rade. 'No person or persons to intrust her with my name, Samuel Balls, for she
> is no longer my right. Then followed the names of 4 witnesses: Samuel Balls,
> M. Bullock (village constable), George Whincop and Robert Sherington (landlord
> of the White Hart).

The ritual of wife-selling, then, consisted of an unwanted wife being taken into the market square of a town with a halter around her neck. Although it would appear that most of the sales had a pre-arranged conclusion (in that the buyer was often already the lover of the woman concerned), she was then auctioned off. A payment was made, usually in cash. But it sometimes involved goods or livestock as in this example from the same newspaper on 29 September 1764:

> Last week a man and his wife falling into discourse with a grazier at Parham Fair,
> the husband offered his wife in exchange for an ox provided he would let him choose
> one out of his drove, the grazier accepted the proposal and the wife readily agreed,

Selling A Wife by Thomas Rowlandson (1756–1827).

accordingly they met the next day and she was delivered with a new halter round her neck and the husband received the bullock which he sold for 6 guineas, it is said the wife has since returned to her husband, they had been married about 10 years.

Even if the wife was happy with the sale, it appears that other women were prepared to stand up for their feminine rights. This report is from the *Bury Post* of 16 May 1821:

Last week a disgraceful circumstance occurred at Sudbury when Henry Frost sold his wife (with the customary halter round her neck) to one Robert Whiting for 2s, but the bargain being offensive to a number of females present they would have given the new bridegroom a summary chastisement had he not taken refuge in a cottage nearby: but when they pursued him he was obliged to make his escape by jumping out of the chamber window.

ॐ

Thomas Tusser was not your average Suffolk farmer. Born over the border in Essex in about 1524, he was a chorister at St Paul's Cathedral before studying at Eton and Cambridge. In fact, he started his career as a court musician but after ten years married and settled down in Cattawade to farm at Braham Hall where he is credited with introducing barley to the area. Not content with learning the art of husbandry (farming), he wrote a long poem in rhyming couplets recording the country year and giving advice on all aspects of good practice. This was published in 1557 under the title *A Hundreth Good Pointes of Husbandrie*. So successful was this book that he enlarged this in his 1573 publication *Five Hundreth Pointes of Good Husbandrie*. In it he includes a curious mix of instructions and observations about farming and country customs, which offer insight into life in Tudor England, as well as recording many terms and proverbs in print for the first time. In this second, expanded book he also includes a few verses giving advice on being a good husband:

> True wedlock is best, for avoiding of sin;
> The bed undefiled, much honour doth win:
> Though love be in choosing, far better than gold,
> Let love come with somewhat, the better to hold.

> Where couples agree not, is rancour and strife,
> Where such be together, is seldom good life;
> Where couples in wedlock do lovely agree,
> There foison [abundance] remaineth, if wisdom there be.

✧ VIRGINS ✧

Walsham le Willows church is home to an unusual and rare object. It hangs from the south arcade 15ft above the ground. It is a disc (probably terracotta) about 0.5in thick and about 1ft in diameter with a small heart moulded at the top. It is possibly in the position in which it was first mounted, intentionally placed above a particular family box pew. When it was made this object formed part of a virgin's crants (or crantz), also known as a maiden's garland or crown.

The word crants offers clues as to the origin of the custom, which may emanate from Germany, the Netherlands and/or Scandinavia (the German for wreath or garland is *krantz*). At funeral processions of unmarried women (and very occasionally men) these garlands, made specifically for the event, were either carried in front of the coffin by another unmarried girl of the same age, or else placed on top of the coffin. In some parts of the country, a garland was placed in the grave and in others it was hung in a prominent position in the church. The garland or crown itself was often a bell-shaped frame of bands of hoops decorated with ribbons, flowers and rosettes made from folded white paper. Sometimes white gloves were included as a sign of the purity of the deceased. As the Walsham le Willows disc

The virgin's crants medallion in Walsham le Willows church. (Tony Scheuregger)

shows, such objects were the centrepiece to the actual crown giving details of the girl. This one gives the 20-year-old's name and her date of death.

In his tragedy *Hamlet*, William Shakespeare refers to the custom in the description of Ophelia's burial (Act V Scene 1):

> … Her death was doubtful,
> And but that great command o'ersways the order,
> She should in ground unsanctified have lodg'd
> Till the last trumpet; for charitable prayers,
> Shards, flints and pebbles should be thrown on her.
> Yet here she is allow'd her virgin crants,
> her maiden strewments, and the bringing home
> Of bell and burial

The priest who utters these words is even doubtful that Ophelia should be given a Christian burial since she had probably take her own life, let alone honouring her with the maiden's garlands.

This medallion is the only survival from a virgin's crants known to survive in Suffolk. Many more exist in their entirety in other churches across the country. But that is not, of course, cause to cast aspersions on Suffolk girls. It is perhaps just one of those quirks of history that the survival of these objects is less in this region. Although perhaps it also points to it being less-widespread a custom in the county.

☙

In the summer of 1854, a penitentiary, designed to help the rehabilitation of fallen women, opened in Shipmeadow, a parish in Suffolk bordering Norfolk although (like most of Suffolk at the time) coming under the Anglican Bishop of Norwich. It was opened, it seems, in response to local demand and was run along similar lines to those already in existence in London. A report urging rescue work in the region said that 'the prostitution in our City [meaning Norwich] has been painfully proverbial'. The category 'fallen women' encompassed both those women who engaged in sexual activity prior to marriage (and had most probably given birth outside wedlock) as well as actual prostitutes. The penitentiary aimed to restore the spiritual and moral health of women whose virtue had been lost. The 'penitents' wore lilac gowns and white caps and carried out their chores in silence.

Although administered by an all-male council of clergy and local landowners, the penitentiary was staffed by a small group of Christian middle-class women. Among them were members of the Crosse and Suckling families who helped found an Anglican community of the Sisters of Mercy at Shipmeadow. Sadly, due to local opposition the community moved over the border into Norfolk, to Ditchingham, where they established themselves as All Hallows. An edition of Kelly's *Directory for Norfolk* of tells us that by 1883 the penitentiary was thriving:

> The House of Mercy, opened in 1859, in conjunction with the Church Penitentiary
> Association, is under the care of the sisterhood of All Hallows, and has for its object
> the reception of women of unchaste lives, from all parts of England; the house is
> a large cruciform building with a beautiful chapel in the head of the cross; it can
> receive 30 penitents; warden, Rev. E. P. Williams; treasurer, Sister Catherine Rotch;
> Miss Lavinia Cross, lady superior.

❖ WEATHER ❖

There is a small iron headstone in the shape of a cross in Thwaite churchyard which bears the words 'Orlando Whistlecraft, weather prophet & poet, born 1810, died 1893'. Intriguing as this inscription is, it rather understates this man's achievements as one of the country's pioneers of meteorology.

As a boy Orlando Whistlecraft was a talented artist and was a largely self-taught scientist. And from an early age he wrote letters to newspapers on all aspects of nature and science. For sixty-six years – from 1827 through to 1892 – he kept a weather diary in Thwaite, recording thermometer and barometer readings. Early publications included *The Climate of England* (which accepted that tornados could hit the country) and *Rural Gleanings*. But his most famous work was started in 1856 when he published the first annual *Weather Almanac* in which he forecasted meteorological conditions for the coming year. In an interview he gave to the *East Anglian Daily Times* in 1892, Whilstecraft explained how the almanac came about: 'I used to study the look of the heavens, and the action of the glass, and so on, and those fortnightly forecasts of mine came so near, so often, that people came to me and said, "You must write an almanac".'

A short piece in the *Framlingham Weekly News* of 4 March 1893 marked his death saying that 'He commenced predicting more than half a century ago his methods being

THE
WEATHER ALMANAC
AND
METEOROLOGICAL AND RURAL HAND-BOOK
FOR
1865,
BEING THE NINTH YEAR OF PUBLICATION,
AND THE TWENTY-NINTH YEAR OF HER MAJESTY'S REIGN.

First   Ten

Edition   Thousand,

of   1865.

THE WEATHER DEPARTMENT BY
ORLANDO WHISTLECRAFT,
METEOROLOGIST,
Author of the "Climate of England," "Rural Gleanings," etc., etc.

LONDON:
SIMPKIN, MARSHALL, & CO., STATIONERS' COURT;
IPSWICH : REES AND GRIFFEN ; BIRMINGHAM : CORNISH BROTHERS ;
BRISTOL : LANDER ; EDINBURGH : MENZIES ; MANCHESTER : JOHN HEYWOOD ;
NORWICH : JARROLD AND SONS ; NORTHAMPTON : NOTCUTT ;
PLYMOUTH : SELLICK ; SOUTHAMPTON : GILBERT ; AND ALL BOOKSELLERS.

Frontispiece from Orlando
Whistlecraft's 1865
Weather Almanac.

altogether primitive compared with the scientific operations of the present day. Nevertheless his predictions were noted for accuracy, and his name will live in East Anglian history as one of her distinguished sons'.

☙❧

As a coastal county, Suffolk residents are aware of the full fury the sea can unleash. And the catastrophic east coast floods of 1953 are still very much fresh in the minds of the many who experienced them. It was one of the worst peacetime disasters ever to hit Britain, striking without warning. Out of the 307 people up and down the east of England who lost their lives as a result of the coastal surge, fifty were in Suffolk; forty-one in Felixstowe alone.

On the night of Saturday, 31 January 1953 a spring tide combined with gales driving down the North Sea raised the water to a dangerous level. The resulting surge was over 2.5m high at its peak and the sea defences were simply inadequate. In Suffolk there was not a single estuary or valley that was not affected by the flooding, which extended to over 20,000 acres of land. Trains on the Ipswich to Lowestoft line through Woodbridge were abandoned as the water reached platform level. And a large swathe of the southern part of the town of Felixstowe was flooded. Up the coast in Southwold, the town was cut off for two days and part of the South Pier was washed away.

Ipswich Town Football Club had been playing away at Torquay that day – sadly losing 4-1 – and arriving back into Ipswich railway station in the early hours of Sunday morning, they were marooned there for nearly five hours. Their ground at Portman Road was under 3ft of water and a pump had to be used to reduce the volume of water in the main stand enclosure. Three weeks later, however, the club hosted a match against the Royal Navy at which all the proceeds went to the East Coast Flood Relief Fund. And regaining some dignity, they beat the sailors 3-1.

✢ WONDERS ✢

Visitors strolling along Cumberland Street in Woodbridge may find themselves staring up at two identical plaster heads over the upper windows of one of the houses. The likeness is none other than an entertainer who called himself Mr Thurton. It was not unusual for such 'wonders' of the Victorian stage to have busts or full-length statues erected on their properties: the ultimate self-publicity stunt! But Mr Thurton appears to have been a highly successful showman in his lifetime, touring the world with his 'Odd Folks' and, later, 'Fresh Faces'. The 1868 issue of an annual register of entertainers carried the following advertisement:

> Mr Thurton having retired for a while from his profession, will resume his performances in the Autumn of the present year, 1868, when he intends producing a new series of sketches, taken from notes and memorandums made during the last 16 years, together with an account of his early days. The whole embellished with elegant costumes, music, magic, song, solo, dance, imitation and ventriloquism.

It appears that Thurton (born John Robert Thurton Smith, the son of a veterinary surgeon) was able to recruit a number of talented artists to perform alongside him, to complement his own skills as a ventriloquist and impersonator. The 'Odd Folks' became a significant draw in town halls and seaside entertainment venues across the globe. Despite his worldwide popularity, he also performed closer to his parental (and then his own) home in Suffolk. The *Bury and Norwich Post* of 11 November 1879 reports on the opening evening of the Haughley Reading Room (a very parochial venue) where Thurton's 'Odd Folks' performed. The paper reports that 'Mr Thurton

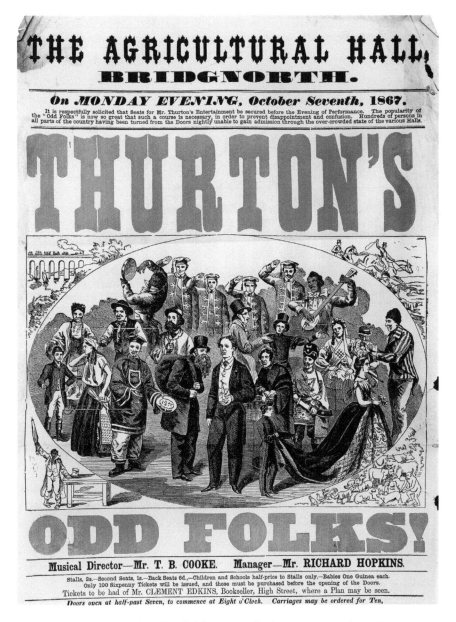

A playbill for Thurton's 'Odd Folks'. (Courtesy of Robertson Davies Library, Toronto. Photographer: Andrew Steeves)

is so general a favourite, especially amongst his Suffolk friends and in his own county that he always meets with a hearty welcome such as that which he received last night from an overflowing audience, which the room could not fully accommodate'.

When John Robert Thurton Smith died in 1886 at the age of 55, he left a personal estate worth a staggering £1,225 (approximately £90,000 today). So it proves that it was not the advent of television that made fortunes for popular entertainers. This extract from an obituary published in the *Bury and Norwich Post* gives us a real flavour of his act:

> Not only was he an unapproached impersonator, but the creator of his own characters … His character of 'Butty Syer' … can hardly be reproduced, unless a new 'Suffolk artist' should arise, for the broad Suffolk of 'Butty's' language can never be mastered except by an intimate acquaintance with every peculiarity of the dialect and its vocal inflections.

๑๐

Enjoyment of such 'wonders' have not been restricted to the Victorian era. In the first half of the twentieth century, the White Hart pub in Boxford was home to a local eccentric and nationwide legend called George 'Tornado' Smith. He has been acknowledged by the British motorcycle industry as the first Englishman to perform the 'Wall of Death' in this country. The 'Wall of Death' is a spectacular but nevertheless highly dangerous form of entertainment where motorcyclists ride horizontally on the inside of a vertical, cylindrical wall. Even more daring was that he performed this stunt accompanied by his pet lioness called Briton. As a cub, the lion would ride on the handlebars of Tornado's bike, but once fully grown she rode in a sidecar.

Tornado's first public appearance was in 1930 in Sweden and on his return to England he set up this country's first 'Wall of Death' at an amusement park in Southend-on-Sea, Essex. Later his wife, nicknamed 'Marjorie Dare', often performed alongside him. Tornado would sometimes ride the wall with a coffin as a side car, complete with a skeleton passenger. And to advertise the forthcoming events, he would be seen travelling the streets on his penny-farthing bicycle handing out flyers. During winter breaks, Tornado, Marjorie and Briton would return to Tornado's home town of Boxford. Here they would put on shows for the residents and it was not uncommon to see Tornado taking Briton for a walk on a lead through the streets.

Sadly Briton did not live to see Tornado's later successes. At the outbreak of the Second World War with the resulting meat shortages, Tornado found that he could not supply the lioness with enough daily meat and so he had no option but to shoot her. He buried his beloved Briton in the courtyard of the

White Hart where her remains still lie. So perhaps, as well as its claim to fame in its connection to Tornado Smith, the public house can boast that it is unique in that it has a lion buried under the car park!

ฉชฉ

Neither were these 'wonders' confined primarily to men. In 1969, Pansy Chinery, a 90-year-old widow, died in an Ipswich nursing home. It was only after her death that her family found a trunk in the attic which contained photographs, programmes, newspaper cuttings, posters and even props relating to her highly successful career as the 'Human Arrow'. Born Frances Elizabeth Mary Murphy (but always known as Pansy), she and her sister ran away to join the circus when their parents died. They joined a troupe called the Flying Zedoras and started an aerial act. In this act, Pansy would be shot from a giant crossbow through the air and through a large paper target. She would be caught on the other side by her sister swinging on a trapeze.

Between 1891 and 1896 the 'Zedora sisters' toured America with Barnum and Bailey's 'Greatest Show on Earth' and wowed the audiences on the other side of the Atlantic. The newspapers there hailed her as 'The crowning miracle of physical and mechanical sensation, surpassing adequate description ... the bravest of all living artists'. The Zedora's Flying Arrow Trapeze Act demanded precise timing, since mistakes could be dangerous. There were frequent accidents, including one in 1897 in Madison Square Gardens when a string was pulled too early and Pansy was knocked unconscious by her crossbow.

Pansy performed until 1916 (when she was 37 years old), later performing as a member of acts including 'Mars and Mars' and 'The Ritz Trio'. She also went on to join a ladder-balancing act called 'The Uniques'. A fitting description of a truly remarkable woman.

⁜ X-FILES ⁜

There is a strange tale which would probably be dismissed as pure fantasy were it not for the fact that it was recorded by one of the most famous chroniclers of Britain. In his *Chronicum Anlicarum* (*The Chronicles of England*), Ralph of Coggeshall records:

The Green Children of Woolpit on the village sign. (Tony Scheuregger)

Another strange thing … happened in Suffolk in the church parish of St Mary of Wulpetes [Woolpit]. A boy was discovered with his sister by some local peasants at the edge of a pit. They looked like other people except for the colour of their skin. Their skin was tinged all over with a green colour. No-one could understand their language.

Ralph was a monk based in Essex who wrote his history between 1187 and 1224. Reputed to have travelled widely throughout East Anglia, he gained much of his information first-hand. And it is thought that he may have been told this story by Sir Richard de Calne, of nearby Wyken Hall, to whom the villagers of Woolpit had taken the children. This was probably because he was the nearest non-native English speaker and they hoped that he might be able to communicate with the pair. Sir Richard took in the children and cared for them.

The chronicle continues to describe how for a long time the children, having been offered all kinds of food, would eat nothing but beans. The boy always appeared tired and ill and died shortly after their discovery. However, the girl grew accustomed to other types of food and lost her green colour completely, returning to the normal, human pink colour. The Green Children of Woolpit as they are known, feature on the village sign as a testament to the popularity of this story. Rather than aliens from outer space, it is possible that they were merely sent on an errand from a nearby village, wandered into the forest and got lost. If they had survived in the woods by eating leaves and berries, the lack of meat and other iron-rich food may have given rise to severe anaemia or Chlorosis (also called Green Sickness) which causes the skin to take on a greenish tinge. Once they ate a normal diet again, the condition would improve. But what about the language problem? In the twelfth century it is conceivable that dialects differed so much from one community to another, that the frightened children could not be easily understood.

❦

Rendlesham Forest has, perhaps, the most unusual waymarked trail in the country. But then it can claim to be the site of the most famous alleged UFO landing in Britain. Over a series of three nights in December 1980, an extraordinary set of incidents occurred, next to two United States Air Force bases: RAF Bentwaters and RAF Woodbridge. It was not just a sighting of some lights in the sky, but an actual 'invasion' of Earth by aliens from outer space. It even prompted the *News of the World* headline 'UFO lands in Suffolk – and that's official'. But we shouldn't just take the word of a tabloid newspaper. There are a number of credible witnesses who gave accounts at the time of the sighting. And many books have been published on the incidents which investigate thoroughly all the evidence. Of course, the sightings have also been explained away as either a complete hoax, a fireball, bright stars or the light from the nearby Orford Ness lighthouse (at that time one of the brightest in the UK). Nevertheless, many people remain convinced that aliens did come to earth in Suffolk one winter.

In the early hours of 26 December 1980, United States military personnel spotted strange lights above Rendlesham Forest. Three men were told to go and investigate, as one of these witnesses explained in his official statement:

> As we went down the east-gate road and the road that leads into the forest, the lights were moving back and they appeared to stop in a bunch of trees … Also, the woods lit up and you could hear the farm animals making a lot of noises, and there was a lot of movement in the woods. All three of us hit the ground and whatever it was started moving back towards the open field … We got up to a fence that separated the trees from the open field. You could see the lights down by a farmer's house. We climbed over the fence and started walking toward the red and blue lights and they just disappeared.

Elaborating further on his colleague's statement, one of the servicemen reported seeing a craft covered in hieroglyphic characters:

> I estimated it to be about three metres tall and about three metres wide at the base … No landing gear was apparent, but it seemed like she was on fixed legs … I moved a little closer … I walked around the craft, and finally, I walked right up to the craft. I noticed the fabric of the shell was more like a smooth, opaque, black glass.

He even drew detailed drawings of the spacecraft to accompany his statement.

The next morning the servicemen returned to the scene. They found, in a small clearing, three small impressions in a triangular pattern, as well as burn marks and broken tree branches. Two days later a senior serviceman and his team were despatched early in the morning who claim they experienced a similar set of events which they recorded. The audio tape, now considered one of the most valuable pieces of evidence, runs for eighteen minutes during which time they describe something like an eye winking at them and beaming a light down to the ground. They also claim to have detected high levels of radiation at the landing site.

In 2005, the Forestry Commission opened a trail in Rendlesham Forest which stops at various places where the servicemen reported to have experienced these extra-terrestrial happenings. And in 2014 a sculpture, representing the UFO as described in witness statements, was placed in the clearing where the spacecraft was supposed to have landed.

❖ XENOPHOBIA ❖

During the First World War, German prisoners of war were held in internment camps across the country. Those prisoners housed in East Anglia were employed in farm work and other manual labour, including clearing rivers. It is difficult to tell from the newspaper reports of these routine events how the locals regarded these Germans. But it appears from a remarkable story of some prisoner-of-war escapees that even our own troops were oblivious to the 'enemy in their midst'. The *East Suffolk Gazette* of 8 May 1917 takes up the story:

> Three escaped German prisoners from Pattishall Internment Camp, Northamptonshire, Corpl. Walter Rivera, Lieut. Gustav Lutz, Sergt.-Major Wilhelm Landes were met by Police-constable Seaman on the Lowestoft road at Southwold on Sunday afternoon. The policeman was in plain clothes. The prisoners' appearance aroused his suspicions, and he challenged them, and then discovered who they were. Police-constable Seaman is to be highly commended for his action in this matter, as he had no information of any prisoners being at large. The story told by the prisoners of their adventures is of exceptional interest. They escaped from the camp during the night … made for the station, and took [a] train next morning, and, not even seeking the privacy of a quiet carriage, travelled for 40 miles with a carriage full of British soldiers, who spent a good deal of the time anathematising the Kaiser and all other Germans. That they should have escaped detection on this journey seems incredible, for the NCO, although wearing a civilian cap, had his field grey overcoat on, and the German service top boots.

The three prisoners of war managed to travel by train, changing trains several times, all the way to Halesworth where they disembarked and walked to Southwold. The following day, they were walking around the town when they were spotted by Constable Seaman:

Their appearance was not to Constable Seaman's liking, and although in plain clothes he stopped them and inquired who they were and what they were doing. The officer's English carried him through the ordeal, but his companions were only able to speak broken English, and on informing the policeman 'that they were Breetish,' he told them they must accompany him, and on that they confessed that they were escaped prisoners.

This incredible story became national news and the vigilant Suffolk policeman was hailed as a hero.

◈⊷

Even on a warm, sunny summer's day, the remote coastal hamlet of Shingle Street has a distinctly eerie feel. The few buildings which do still exist, strung along the top of the beach, are under threat from the sea. A 2004 report suggested that Shingle Street could disappear completely within twenty years if sea defences were not erected. It was also the scene of one of the most mysterious and (to date) unexplained incidents of the Second World War.

After the Dunkirk evacuation in 1940, Britain was on high alert in case of a German invasion and on 7 September 1940 the 'Cromwell' code – which warned of an imminent invasion – was given in error. As a result, there were numerous rumours of landings by sea and German parachutists. And it was around this time that stories began to emerge of a large number of badly

Shingle Street. (Tony Scheuregger)

burnt, dead German troops having been washed up on shores in the south-east, including at Shingle Street. Like other civilians living along the coastal areas, residents of Shingle Street had already been evacuated because of the threat of invasion. And so, supposedly, there were no non-military eyewitnesses to the incident. However, non-official accounts have continued to trickle out ever since.

Until all the government files relating to the event are in the public domain, we shall not know the real story. But several theories have emerged as to what happened. It is possible that, indeed, a German invasion force was foiled in their attempt to land on British soil, repelled by flame throwers which we know were deployed along the Suffolk coast. Some believe that the bodies were actually British servicemen killed in a training exercise that went wrong. Or was the story of dead Germans all just government propaganda to stir up patriotism? However, the last explanation does not account for various civilian sightings of the bodies which have been reported over the years. Whatever the truth is, and whenever it is revealed, one thing is certain: the desolate shingle beach is not about to give up its secrets.

✤ YANKS ✤

Suffolk rightly claims to have been the home of many of the founding fathers of the United States of America. One of the now recognised unsung pioneers from the county is Captain Bartholomew Gosnold. Gosnold was born in Grundisburgh in 1571 and his family seat was nearby at Otley Hall. He captained two expeditions to the New World. The first was in 1602 when he founded and named Cape Cod, Martha's Vineyard (named after his daughter) and Cutty Hunk. The second was in 1607 when he was the prime mover in the formation of the first English-speaking colony in Jamestown (now known as Virginia). Gosnold died only four months after landing in America the second time.

In 2003, it was announced that an archaeological dig at Jamestown had discovered the likely location of Gosnold's grave. Two years later, after trying unsuccessfully to trace any living descendants, experts obtained permission from the Diocese of St Edmundsbury and Ipswich to exhume the remains of two British women buried in Suffolk churchyards; in Shelley and in Stowmarket. They were Elizabeth Tilney, Gosnold's sister, and his niece, Katherine Blackerby. In the event, only one set of remains were located and samples of bone were taken. Sadly, DNA analysis proved inconclusive, probably because the body located beneath the church floor was not that of Elizabeth Tilney.

In July 2006, a Native American chief visited Otley Hall to pay homage to Bartholomew Gosnold. It is believed that his first encounter with other human life within the New World was with the Rappahannock Indians. During her visit and dressed in her traditional regalia of a bleached and tasselled buckskin dress and formal headdress intricately decorated with glass beads, Chief Anne G. Richardson of the Rappahannock tribe said:

> In our tribal spirituality we have something called the circle of life. We believe that from the time we were born to the time we die that we take a journey of life and return back to that place. This visit is the fulfilment of the circle of what has taken place 400 years ago.

ଶ⚬ଵ

In one corner of the Abbey Gardens in Bury St Edmunds, in the shadow of the cathedral's new Millennium Tower and the ruins of the west front of the abbey, is the Appleby Rose Garden. Rather than being named after a town dignitary or a former abbot of the abbey itself, the title is derived from an American serviceman who spent just eight months in Suffolk during the Second World War.

John Tate Appleby was born in Arkansas where his family were farmers. He had travelled around Europe as a reporter for the *Washington Post* and when America had joined the Allies in the war against Germany, he had enlisted in the 8th United States Army Air Force as a trainer. The 8th United States Army Air Force had been in East Anglia since November 1942 and flew a total of 493 operational missions out of the area. John Appleby was posted to RAF Lavenham (also known as Cockfield), as it happened only a matter of weeks before Germany's unconditional surrender in May 1945. During that summer, Appleby was able to travel around Suffolk by bicycle, exploring the countryside and pursuing his new hobby of brass rubbing. And it is his impressions of the places he visited that he committed to paper after the war, publishing it under the title *Suffolk Summer*. The book was a huge hit and since its publication in 1948 has been reprinted many times.

In the book, Appleby describes his first impression of the county: 'As I wandered about the field, which lay sprawled over several miles of countryside, I got my first good look at the Suffolk scene. The American eye is struck first of all by the dazzling greenness of the fields and by the beauty of the hedgerows.' His warm, evocative recollections of his summer in Suffolk provide us with snapshots of rural life at the end of the Second World War. He was also clearly deeply in love with the county he found himself in that summer:

The Appleby Rose Garden in Bury St Edmunds. (Tony Scheuregger)

The English landscape at its subtlest and loveliest is to be seen in the County of Suffolk. I can say this with dogmatic certainty because it is the only county in England that I can pretend to know. Furthermore, the people of Suffolk themselves tell me this, and I know it must be so.

And so taken was Appleby with his time in Suffolk that he donated all the royalties he received from *Suffolk Summer* to the creation of a rose garden in the Abbey Gardens on the site of an old orchard.

The Appleby Rose Garden has sixteen rose beds with some 400 rose bushes of all kinds. Alongside ordinary park benches is a rather unusual one made from the wing of a Flying Fortress bomber aircraft. There is also a memorial stone in recognition of the many American servicemen and women stationed in Suffolk.

⚜ YEOMAN ⚜

The Suffolk landscape, economy and employment have been dominated by farming for centuries. There have been many commentators and agricultural reformers who have influenced farming practice in the country, but perhaps none greater than Arthur Young. Born in 1741, the son of a Suffolk clergyman, Young forged an early career as a novelist. On inheriting his father's Suffolk estate in 1759, and through becoming manager of a farm in Essex, Young emerged as a tireless propagandist for agricultural improvement, constantly experimenting with new farming methods. In essence, therefore, he became a yeoman (a gentleman farmer).

Arthur Young spent a great deal of his life travelling in this country and in France, and these journeys were the basis for a forty-five-volume series of books (*Annals in Agriculture*) describing changes in both agriculture and wider social and political developments. In 1793 when the government created its first Board of Agriculture, Young became its secretary. In this role he directed further major agricultural surveys.

Young's *General View of the Agriculture of the County of Suffolk* was published in 1813. It provides us with a detailed snapshot of the state of the county's farming. In the chapter detailing livestock, he gives an account of rabbit farming which had profited from providing rabbits to the London markets, in particular during the Napoleonic Wars. This is what he says:

There are many warrens in Suffolk, especially in the western sand district; but within the twenty last years, great tracts of them have been ploughed up, and converted to the much better use of yielding corn, mutton and wool. From this circumstance, has arisen the great increase of the price for these furs. Thirty years ago, the skins were at five shillings a dozen; they gradually rose to twelve shillings; but, since the commencement of the present war, have fallen to seven shillings … There is one [warren] near Brandon, which is said to return above forty thousand rabbits in a year.

☙❧

It is widely believed that it was Arthur Young (see above) who had the original idea for an organised, mounted and armed volunteer force in Suffolk. On 1 February 1793, France declared war on Britain and there was a real fear of a French invasion on our shores. The Royal Navy defended the coastline from the sea. But up to this point, our home defence had relied on the militia whereby each county provided a quota of men raised by ballot from every parish.

However, because the government was also worried about a revolution within Britain itself, militia regiments were not allowed to serve in their home county as there was a worry that they might sympathise with any local rebels. Such were the concerns that King George III issued a royal proclamation calling on his subjects to resist radical attempts to subvert legitimate government. Suffolk loyalists responded by forming a Loyal Association 'for the purposes of supporting our most excellent constitution in Church and State and preserving liberty and property against Levellers, Republicans and abettors of the designs of France against this country'; not a terribly snappy title, but nevertheless providing a focus for loyalist activity.

The formal establishment of the Loyal Suffolk Yeomanry Cavalry took place in 1794. Yeomanry was a term used countrywide for such forces springing up at this time, which reflected the fact that it comprised mainly landowners, wealthy farmers and prominent local tradesmen. New recruits were required to find their own horses and clothing while the government provided arms.

Alongside this Suffolk-wide body, many other more local volunteer forces appeared, most instigated by local landowners anxious, no doubt, to get noticed by senior figures in the government and even the monarch. One such company which is well documented and has been meticulously researched is the Loyal Worlingworth Volunteer Corps. This was in existence from 1 June 1798 to 30 April 1802 and was instigated by John Henniker-Major, the son of Sir John Henniker whose family owned extensive estates in Suffolk at Thornham,

Worlingworth and elsewhere. Its inaugural meeting was held in the Swan Inn in Worllngworth and a surviving muster roll lists ninety men who signed up to serve in the infantry. At this meeting it was resolved unanimously that the corps be

> … raised, exercised and employed in any place within the Parishes abovementioned [Worlingworth, Southolt, Athelington, Horham, Wilby, Brundish, Saxstead, Bedfield and Tannington], government finding arms and accoutrements, with such proportion of ammunition as may be necessary for the use of the Corps, government also finding a Drill Serjeant, a Drummer and a Fifer.

It was also agreed that the corps arrange appropriate dress for their men. It is not known precisely how the volunteers were kitted out uniform-wise. But several recent finds by metal detectorists have included tunic buttons with the words

A tunic button bearing the words 'Worlingworth Volunteers'.
(Courtesy of Geoff Robinson)

'Worlingworth Volunteers' on them together with a heart surrounded by nine hands. This points to a standard dress, perhaps paid for by John Henniker-Major. And although no contemporary pictures exist of the volunteer force, there is a surviving painting in the Ipswich Museum of Captain Henniker-Major in his full dress uniform of blue coat with red collar, white breeches, black boots and a pink sash tied round his waist. His sword strap shows the same insignia of heart and hands as appear on the tunic buttons. He is depicted holding the bridle of a black horse. This painting is one of very few which exist of a Suffolk Napoleonic volunteer and is therefore of great historic value. It is currently in poor condition. A local fund-raising campaign is underway to raise the necessary finance needed for the painting to undergo extensive conservation.

⚜ ZEPPELIN ⚜

Before the twentieth century, the civilian population of Britain had been largely unaffected by war. Overseas wars rarely touched our shores. But the First World War changed all that, with the advent of war from the skies. The eastern counties were particularly vulnerable to air attacks by the dreaded Zeppelin. These airships had been designed and developed by Count von Zeppelin in 1900 as a comfortable craft for passenger air travel. Soon afterwards, however, seized on by the German military as potential weapons of war, these 190m-long, hydrogen-filled, rugby ball-shaped balloons soon became an object which struck fear into the British people. They could travel at around 85mph and carry up to 2 tonnes of bombs.

The first Zeppelin bombing raid over the country was on Great Yarmouth and King's Lynn in Norfolk in January 1915. But it was not long until Suffolk, too, received some devastating blows. Ipswich, Lowestoft and Bury St Edmunds were all bombed in April 1915. Each raid caused considerable damage to both houses and businesses in the town centres, although relatively few casualties were sustained.

And then on the night of 12 August 1915, Woodbridge was targeted by Zeppelin *L10*. Over one hundred houses were damaged or destroyed and six people lost their lives; a further twenty-three were injured. Those killed included a 17 year old who delayed leaving his house with the rest of his family when the attack began in order to finish a cup of cocoa; a young married couple, who left behind three children, including an infant only a few weeks old; and a 50-year-old volunteer fireman, killed as he hurried towards the fire station to help the rescue effort. Funerals for the victims took place at Woodbridge Cemetery on 17 August 1915. The whole town closed for business to pay their respects to the victims, and crowds thronged the streets to observe the funeral procession. The 10th London Regiment, which was stationed in the town, provided a military escort, a band, bugles, and firing party for the burials.

A porcelain piece commemorating the Bury St Edmunds Zeppelin raid in April 1915. (Courtesy of Martyn Taylor and David Addy)

Many towns which suffered at the hands of the dreaded Zeppelin commissioned commemorative porcelain from W.H. Goss of Staffordshire. These pieces were about an inch tall and were shaped like an incendiary bomb. The town's coat of arms was prominent on the main body and the base carried an inscription. An existing porcelain piece commemorating the Bury St Edmunds raid reads: 'Model of German Bomb dropped on Bury St Edmunds from a Zeppelin 30 April 1915.'

⚬╉⚬

The residents of the small village of Theberton, a few miles from the sea, were awoken in the early hours of Sunday, 17 June 1917 not by an airborne raid but by the noise and commotion following the shooting down of the Zeppelin *L48*. The *L48* was one of the new type of Zeppelin known as 'Height Climbers'. They were made from thinner-gauge material than the earlier models (making it much riskier to fly), had one less engine and carried no armaments.

The *L48* had flown over towards the east coast in the company of another Zeppelin. They had already dropped bombs on Martlesham (with little effect) when they came under fire by British anti-aircraft guns on shore and on ships at sea. The Zeppelin had intended to attack Harwich next but were deterred by their onslaught. British planes were then despatched to engage the Zeppelin and the *L48*, being hit, burst into flames at the tail. The airship fell to the ground, taking up to five minutes to descend to ground level. Many of the crew were trapped in the burning wreckage and perished there. Other occupants jumped out before the Zeppelin hit the ground, although did not survive the fall. There were only three survivors. The wreckage of the great flying ship was a major spectacle for local people and until it was removed was heavily guarded by military personnel to deter souvenir hunters. The scorch marks made by

A piece of Zeppelin *L48* shot down over Suffolk in June 1917. (Tony Scheuregger)

the burning Zeppelin can still be seen today in the ploughed field on modern satellite photographs of the area.

Fourteen bodies were recovered from the burnt-out shell. An inquest was held outside the local farmhouse, and a funeral arranged for the dead. The bodies were borne on gun carriages and army wagons. They were buried in one grave in Theberton churchyard. Later they were transferred to Cannock Chase cemetery in Staffordshire in which most of the German dead of both world wars now rest. Inside the porch of the church, however, there remains a surprisingly large piece of the shot-down Zeppelin *L48*.

Bibliography

Books

Archer, J., *A Prison Diary Volume III: Heaven* (Pan, London, 2005)

Badham, S. and Statham, M., *Jankyn Smith of Bury St Edmunds and his Brass* (Bury Record Office, Bury St Edmunds, 2012)

Bance, P., *The Duleep Singhs: The Photograph Album of Queen Victoria's Maharajah* (Sutton, Stroud, 2004)

Bettley, J. and Pevsner, N., *The Buildings of England, Suffolk: East* (Yale, London, 2015)

Bettley, J. and Pevsner, N., *The Buildings of England, Suffolk: West* (Yale, London, 2015)

Briggs, J., *Curiosities of Suffolk: A County Guide to the Unusual* (John Nickalls, Norfolk, 2005)

Champion, M., *Medieval Graffiti: The Lost Voices of England's Churches* (Ebury Press, London, 2015)

Cockayne, E. and Jone, R., *The Green Children of Woolpit* (The Authors, n.d.)

Coleman, M., *The 16th-century household secrets of Catherine Tollemache at Helmingham Hall* (Phillimore, Andover, 2012)

De Mille, A.O., *One Man's Dream: The Story behind G. Stuart Ogilvie and the Creation of Thorpeness* (Nostalgia Publications, Dereham, 1996)

Dymond, D and Martin, E., (eds), *An Historical Atlas of Suffolk* 3rd edition, revised and enlarged (The Archaeology Service, Suffolk County Council, Ipswich, 1999)

Dymond, D., *Parson and People in a Suffolk Village: Richard Cobbold's Wortham, 1824-77* (Wortham Research Group and Suffolk Family History Society, Wortham, 2008)

Elliiott, G., *Hidden Suffolk* (Countryside Books, Newbury, 2000)

Evans, G.E., *The Pattern under the Plough: Aspects of the Folklife of East Anglia* (Little Toller, Dorset, 2013)

Foley, M., *Front-line Suffolk* (Sutton, Stroud, 2007)

Halliday, R., *Suffolk Strange But True* (The History Press, Stroud, 2008)

Hardy, S.M., *The Cretingham Murder* (S.M. Hardy, Tattingstone, 2000)

Hinchley, A. and Macready, J., *A Tale of Two Rivers: An Illustrated Walking Guide to the Rivers and Water Meadows of Bury St Edmunds* (Bury Water Meadows Group, 2015)

Jennings, P., *Haunted Suffolk* (The History Press, Stroud, 2006)

La Rochefoucauld, F.D. and Scarfe, N., *A Frenchman's Year in Suffolk, 1784* (Boydell, Woodbridge, 2011)

Meldola, R. and White, W., *Report on the East Anglian Earthquake of April 22nd 1884* (Macmillan, London, 1885)

Orridge, J., *Description of the Gaol at Bury St Edmunds* (Rodwell & Martin, London, 1819)

Pope, N. with Burroughs, J. and Penniston, J., *Encounter in Rendlesham Forest* (Thistle, London, 2014)

Puttick, B., *Ghosts of Suffolk* (Countryside Books, Newbury, 1998)

Reeve, C., *A Straunge and Terrible Wunder: The Story of the Black Dog of Bungay* (Morrow, Bungay, 1988)

Roberts, W. M., *Lost Country Houses of Suffolk* (Boydell, Woodbridge, 2010)

Sanford, M., *A Flora of Suffolk* (Suffolk Naturalists Society, Ipswich, 2010)

Sign, N. and Thomas, M., *The Loyal Suffolk Hussars: The History of the Suffolk Yeomanry 1794-1967* (Helion, Solihull, 2012)

Statham, M., *The Book of Bury St Edmunds* (Baron Birch, Towcester, 1996)

Storey, N.R., *The Little Book of Suffolk* (The History Press, Stroud, 2013)

Twinch, C., *Great Suffolk Stories* (Fort, Ayr, 2003)

Twinch, C., *The Little Book of Suffolk* (Breedon Books, Derby, 2007)

Windsor, W.W., Duchess of, *The Heart had its Reason: The Memoirs of The Duchess of Windsor* (Michael Joseph, London, 1956)

Wright, P., *Frolic, Fervour and Fornication: An Alternative History of Suffolk* (Pawprint Publishing, Stowmarket, 2014)

Websites

The following websites used in researching this book were accessible at the time of writing (November 2015). Where I used Wikipedia website entries, I used fully sourced material or ensured that I verified details with a further source.

en.wikipedia.org

www.aspall.co.uk

www.ballads.bodleian.ox.ac.uk

www.bbc.co.uk

www.books.google.co.uk

www.british-history.ac.uk

www.britishnewspaperarchive.co.uk

www.buildingconservation.com

www.eadt.co.uk

www.earlsoham.org

www.foxearth.org.uk

www.glemsford.org.uk

www.haverhill-uk.com

www.hct.org.uk

www.landmarktrust.org.uk

www.little-saxham.suffolk.gov.uk/history/hall.shtml

www.longshopmuseum.co.uk

milestones.megalithia.com

www.myweb.tiscali.co.uk/redgravehistory

www.naylandconservation.org.uk

www.ness-point.co.uk

www.nhrm.co.uk

www.old-glory.org.uk

www.pipwright.com

www.smuggling.co.uk

www.stedmundsburychronicle.co.uk

www.stedscathedral.co.uk

www.suffolkchurches.co.uk

www.suffolkwildlifetrust.org

www.summerhillschool.co.uk

www.thecasepubbentley.co.uk

www.thosewhowillnotbedrowned.wordpress.com

www.trinityhouse.co.uk

www.ucshistory.wordpress.com

www.vam.ac.uk

www.visionofbritain.org.uk

www.westsuffolk.gov.uk

Periodicals

I consulted a large number of articles from the following periodicals which are too numerous to list in full. I am grateful to the authors and editors of these journals for their thorough research on which I have been able to draw.

Proceedings of the Suffolk Institute of Archaeology and History
  (see www.suffolkinstitute.org.uk)
Suffolk Fair (R.F. Eastern Ltd)
Suffolk Review: Bulletin of the Suffolk Local History Council (see www.slhc.org.uk)

About the Author

Although SARAH E. DOIG was born in Hertfordshire, she considers herself a Suffolk girl. When she was a year old, Sarah moved with her family first to Mildenhall and then to Bury St Edmunds where she was educated. Leaving Suffolk initially to attend university, Sarah found herself away from the county she considered home for some twenty-seven years.

After having travelled the world during her twenty-year career in the Foreign and Commonwealth Office, Sarah could no longer resist the strong pull back to Suffolk. She therefore completely reinvented herself as a self-employed genealogist, local historian, writer and speaker, drawing on her postgraduate training in information studies as well as the many challenges she had faced in briefing government ministers and royalty alike in her former role. And not being daunted by her now heavy workload, Sarah also plays music professionally as part of an early music trio.

Sarah's website is: www.ancestral-heritage.co.uk

The destination for history
www.thehistorypress.co.uk